Alder			
Ash			
Beech			
Elm			
Fir			
Larch		·55	
Oak		·75	·33	3·0
„ heart of		1·17	sinks	cannot be used
Pine		·40 to ·63	1·50 to ·60	0·7 to 1·7
Poplar		·33	1·83	5·6
Willow		·59	·70	1·4

Fig. 2.

Fig. 1.

A	dul	pal
adv	eve	per
app	fin	ple
bal	gin	pre
bil	hee	pro
bre	imp	que
cap	int	rec
chi	k	reg
col	lan	ris
com	mac	sab
cra	mil	sca

The Art of Rough Travel

From the Peculiar
to the Practical

Advice from a
19th-Century Explorer

Sir Francis Galton

THE MOUNTAINEERS BOOKS is the nonprofit
publishing arm of The Mountaineers Club, an organization
founded in 1906 and dedicated to the exploration, preservation,
and enjoyment of outdoor and wilderness areas.

1001 SW Klickitat Way, Suite 201, Seattle, WA 98134

ISBN 1-59485-058-5
© 2006 by The Mountaineers Books

First edition, 2006

Manufactured in the United States of America

Editor: Kitty Harmon/www.tributarybooks.com
Cover and interior design: Jane Jeszeck/www.jigsawseattle.com

 Printed on recycled paper

Contents

6 INTRODUCTION

11 PREPARATORY INQUIRIES

16 OUTFIT

19 CLOTHING

28 BEASTS OF BURDEN

39 CLIMBING AND MOUNTAINEERING

46 SWIMMING

52 RAFTS AND BOATS

64 FORDS AND BRIDGES

67 WATER FOR DRINKING

78 FOOD

92 GAME

103 FISHING

106 FIRE

113 BEDDING

119 BIVOUAC

127 TENTS

134 BUSH REMEDIES

140 MEASUREMENTS

145 WAYFINDING

158 SIGNALS.

161 CACHES

164 MISCELLANY

171 ON CONCLUDING THE JOURNEY

175 INDEX OF PERSONAGES, PLACES
AND PEOPLES

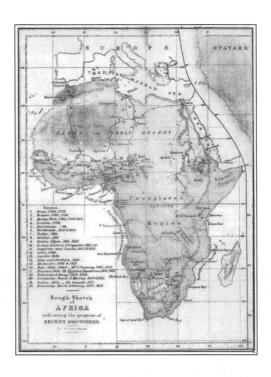

Rough Sketch
of
AFRICA
indicating the progress of
RECENT DISCOVERIES.

The idea of the work occurred to me when exploring South-western Africa in 1850-51. I felt acutely at that time the impossibility of obtaining sufficient information on the subjects of which it treats; for though the natives of that country taught me a great deal, it was obvious that their acquaintance with bush lore was exceedingly partial and limited. Then remembering how the traditional maxims and methods of traveling in each country differ from those of others, and how every traveler discovers some useful contrivances for himself, it appeared to me, that I should do welcome service to all who have to roughit—whether explorers, emigrants, missionaries, or soldiers—by collecting the scattered experiences of many such persons in various circumstances, collating them, examining into their principles, and deducing from them what might fairly be called an "Art of Travel." To this end, on my return home, I searched through a vast number of geographical works, I sought information from numerous travelers of distinction, and I made a point of re-testing, in every needful case, what I had read or learned by hearsay.

—Sir Francis Galton,
from the original introduction

EDITOR'S INTRODUCTION

*I*t is a pleasure to introduce a new, abridged edition of Sir Francis Galton's classic handbook for explorers, originally titled *The Art of Travel: Shifts and Contrivances in Wild Countries.* The book is a masterpiece of the Victorian age, a precise (if not always concise) guide to avoiding or extricating yourself from all manner of trying circumstances—such as starvation, attacks by marauders, the oncoming rush of an enraged animal, and so forth. This would be the "practical" advice to which the publisher's new subtitle alludes. The book also provides "peculiar" nuggets of wisdom for maintaining civilized standards in the rudest of conditions: adding a dressing gown and slippers to your provisions, for example, along with an umbrella and, perhaps, your wife.

The first edition of the book was published in London in 1855, when seemingly any white male with a taste for adventure, a strong constitution, and a bit of backing could make a name for himself by investigating some untamed patch of earth. On the basis of conversation with a few members of the Royal Geographic Society, Galton settled on South-West Africa (now Namibia) and spent two years heading a carefully planned expedition there. He proved an assiduous data gatherer and reporter and, once home, chronicled his adventures for a book-buying audience hungry for descriptions of far-flung locations. As Galton wrote in his autobiography some fifty years later, readers since that time

...need some effort of imagination to put themselves into the mental positions of those who were living in [the mid-19th century]. Blank spaces in the map of the world were then both large and numerous, and the positions of many towns, rivers, and notable districts were untrustworthy. The whole interior of South Africa and much of that of North Africa were quite unknown to civilized man. Similarly as regards that of the great continent of Australia. The unknown geography of the North Polar regions preserved some of the earlier glamour attached to the possibility of finding a navigable north-west passage from England to China, which inspection of the globe shows to be far shorter than that round the Cape. The South Polar regions had only been touched here and there. The geography of Central Asia was in great confusion, the true position of many places familiar in ancient history being most uncertain, while vast areas remained wholly unexplored, in the common sense of that word. It was a time when the ideas of persons interested in geography were in a justifiable state of ferment.

Galton was quite happy to have discovered his own geographic interests in this frothy time. Instead of setting out again, however, he determined he could make another kind of contribution to the explorers' set. Galton had all the benefits of a top-rate education, connections, and a bankroll sufficient to apply them as he wished. He also possessed the Victorian passion for order and "the right way to go about a thing" that led him to compile the knowledge of explorers who had gone before, for the benefit of those who would follow. After all, once having determined a proper bush skill—how to handle an elephant, avoid cobras, pull teeth, find water, keep watch, or pass through hostile country—wouldn't one want to share it?

It is inspiring to imagine oneself in Galton's position as a young man with a world of adventure at his feet—and then, when the adventuring had been enough, sinking into a leather armchair at the Royal Geographic Society to gather survival tactics and tidbits of native lore from peripatetic colleagues. Throughout *The Art of Rough Travel* Galton refers to sources like "Captain Burton" or "Mr. Atkinson" or "FitzRoy" as if they are just over there, in the next circle of club chairs. While the geographic world was large, the society of its explorers was small. Indeed, you can amuse yourself using the thumbnail biographies of explorers added to this edition of the book to play a lively game of Six Degrees of Sir Francis Bacon...er, Sir Francis Galton.

To give Galton his due, he apparently didn't spend much time loafing in club chairs, for he accomplished quite a bit in his lifetime. He was a half-cousin of Charles Darwin, with a similar scientific curiosity and the means to indulge it. In addition to his geographic projects, Galton made significant contributions to the fields of meteorology (discovering the anticyclone), statistics (helping to develop biometrics), psychology (quantifying mental imagery), and forensics (establishing the use of fingerprints for personal identification). In later life, greatly influenced by Darwin's evolutionary theory, Galton delved into the study of human hereditary traits. He was the originator of twin studies and the founder of eugenics (a term he coined, meaning "good in birth"), a distinction tarnished by pursuits of racial purity that followed his death.

Galton wrote numerous scientific papers, journal

articles, and twenty books, of which *The Art of Travel* was the most successful, widely read in many editions. The beauty of this book (and the decision of The Mountaineers Books to bring it back in an updated form) is the density of know-how it contains. We may not have much cause for knowing, today, how to make an oven out of an anthill, or train an ox to take a saddle, or cache jewels within an incision in your arm. Still, the book imbues the reader with a can-do, make-do, derring-do spirit useful in travel situations and life in general. (I certainly wouldn't want to be a contestant on "Survivor" without a copy stuffed into my bikini.)

In its time no explorer would have left home without *The Art of Travel*. With Galton's steady voice in your ear, you will feel that you, too, might endeavor to bivouac in hostile country, manage a horde of bearers, or walk a straight line through the forest. Even, perhaps, from the safety of your own fireside armchair.

—*Kitty Harmon, editor*

A NOTE ON THE TEXT

The text is an adaptation of the fifth edition, the final edition prepared by Galton in 1872. I have cut approximately one third of the text and in several cases combined original chapters to make the overall work more accessible. Much or all of the original's sections on firearms, the nutritional content of foods, flashing signals, and "management of savages" have been left out. Other sections have been condensed, and I have updated place names, Americanized British spellings, and tamed an enthusiasm for hyphens and commas. Nothing was added to the main text or the sidebar material other than the vertically bracketed mini-biographies of most of the men Galton mentions as sources of information in his text. A list of all the names appears in an index on page 175, with boldfaced page numbers indicating the location of biographies. Regrettably, I was unable to find information about a handful of Galton's informants.

PREPARATORY INQUIRIES

ADVANTAGES OF TRAVEL.

REPUTED DANGERS OF TRAVEL.

CONDITIONS OF SUCCESS AND FAILURE IN TRAVEL.

PHYSICAL STRENGTH.

GOOD TEMPER.

SIZE OF PARTY.

To those who meditate travel: If you have health, a great craving for adventure, at least a moderate fortune, and can set your heart on a definite object, which old travelers do not think impracticable, then—travel by all means. If, in addition to these qualifications, you have scientific taste and knowledge, I believe that no career, in time of peace, can offer to you more advantages than that of a traveler. If you have not independent means, you may still turn traveling to excellent account; for experience shows it often leads to promotion, nay, some men support themselves by travel. They explore pasture land in Australia, they hunt for ivory in Africa, they collect specimens of natural history for sale, or they wander as artists.

ADVANTAGES OF TRAVEL.

It is no slight advantage to a young man to have the opportunity for distinction which travel affords. If he plans his journey among scenes and places likely to interest the stay-at-home public, he will probably achieve a reputation that might well be envied by wiser men who have not had his opportunities.

The scientific advantages of travel are enormous to a man prepared to profit by them. He sees nature working by herself, without the interference of human intelligence; and he sees her from new points of view; he has also undisturbed leisure for the problems which perpetually attract his attention

He sees nature working by herself, without the interference of human intelligence

by their novelty. The consequence is, that though scientific travelers are comparatively few, yet out of their ranks a large proportion of the leaders in all branches of science has been supplied. It is one of the most grateful results of a journey to the young traveler to find himself admitted, on the ground of his having so much of special interest to relate, into the society of men with whose names he had long been familiar, and whom he had reverenced as his heroes.

REPUTED DANGERS OF TRAVEL.

A young man of good constitution, who is bound on an enterprise sanctioned by experienced travelers, does not run very great risks. Let those who doubt refer to the history of the various expeditions encouraged by the Royal Geographical Society, and they will see how few deaths have occurred; and of those deaths how small a proportion among young travelers.

CONDITIONS OF SUCCESS AND FAILURE IN TRAVEL.

An exploring expedition is daily exposed to a succession of accidents, any one of which might be fatal to its further progress. The cattle may at any time stray, die, or be stolen; water may not be reached, and they may perish; one or more of the men may become seriously ill, or the party may be attacked by natives. Hence the success of the expedition depends on a chain of eventualities, each link of which must be a success; for if one link fails, at that point, there must be an end of further advance. It is therefore well, especially at the outset of a long journey, not to go hurriedly to work, nor to push

☞ Savages rarely murder newcomers; they fear their guns, and have a superstitious awe of the white man's power: they require time to discover that he is not very different to themselves, and easily to be made away with.

☞ Ordinary fevers are seldom fatal to the sound and elastic constitution of youth, which usually has power to resist the adverse influences of two or three years of wild life.

forward too thoughtlessly. Give the men and cattle time to become acclimatized, make the bush your home, and avoid unnecessary hardships.

Interest yourself chiefly in the progress of your journey, and do not look forward to its end with eagerness. It is better to think of a return to civilization not as an end to hardship and a haven from ill, but as a close to an adventurous and pleasant life. In this way, risking little, and insensibly creeping on, you will make connections and learn the capabilities of the country as you advance; all which will be found invaluable in the case of a hurried or disastrous return. And thus, when some months have passed by, you will look back with surprise on the great distance traveled over; for if you average only 3 miles a day, at the end of the year you will have advanced twelve hundred, which is a very considerable exploration. The fable of the tortoise and the hare is peculiarly applicable to travelers over wide and unknown tracts. It is a very high merit to accomplish a long exploration without loss of health, of papers, or even of comfort.

It is better to think of a return to civilization not as an end to hardship and a haven from ill, but as a close to an adventurous and pleasant life

PHYSICAL STRENGTH.

Powerful men do not necessarily make the most eminent travelers; it is rather those who take the most interest in their work that succeed the best. As a huntsman says, "it is the nose that gives speed to the hound."

Strength of women. I believe there are few greater popular errors than the idea we have mainly derived from chivalrous times, that woman is a weakly creature. I suppose that in the days of

☞ It is in the nature of women to be fond of carrying weights; you may see them in omnibuses and carriages, always preferring to hold their baskets or their babies on their knees, to setting them down on the seats by their sides. A woman, whose modern dress includes I know not how many cubic feet of space, has hardly ever pockets of a sufficient size to carry small articles; for she prefers to load her hands with a bag or other weighty object.

baronial castles, when crowds of people herded together like pigs within the narrow enclosures of a fortification, and the ladies did nothing but needle-work in their boudoirs, the mode of life was very prejudicial to their nervous system and muscular powers. The women suffered from the effects of ill ventilation and bad drainage, and had none of the counteracting advantages of the military life that was led by the males. Consequently women really became the helpless dolls that they were considered to be, and which it is still the fashion to consider them. It always seems to me that a hard-worked woman is better and happier for her work.

GOOD TEMPER.

Tedious journeys are apt to make companions irritable one to another; but under hard circumstances, a traveler does his duty best who doubles his kindliness of manner to those about him, and takes harsh words gently, and without retort. He should make it a point of duty to do so. It is at those times very superfluous to show too much punctiliousness about keeping up one's dignity and so forth; since the difficulty lies not in taking up quarrels, but in avoiding them.

SIZE OF PARTY.

The best size for a party depends on many considerations. It should admit of being divided into two parts, each strong enough to take care of itself, and in each of which is one person at least able to write a letter, which bush servants, excellent in every other particular, are too often unable to do. In travel through a disorganized country, where there are small chiefs and bands of marauders, a large party is necessary; in other cases small parties succeed better than large ones; they excite less fear, do not eat up the country, and are less delayed by illness.

Solitary travelers. Neither sleepy nor deaf men are fit to travel quite alone. It is remarkable how often the qualities of wakefulness and watchfulness stand every party in good stead.

Natives' wives. If some of the natives take their wives, it gives great life to the party. They are of very great service and cause no delay; for the body of a caravan must always travel at a foot's pace, and a woman will endure a long journey nearly as well as a man, and certainly better than a horse or a bullock. They are invaluable in picking up and retailing information and hearsay gossip, which will give clues to much of importance, that, unassisted, you might miss. Mr. Hearne, ◆ the American traveler of the last century, in his charming book, writes as follows:

> *The very plan which, by the desire of the Governor, we pursued, of not taking any women with us on the journey, was, as the chief said, the principal thing that occasioned all our want: 'for,' said he, 'when all the men are heavy laden, they can neither hunt nor travel to any considerable distance; and if they meet with any success in hunting, who is to carry the produce of the labor?' 'Women,' said he, 'were made for labor: one of them can carry or haul as much as two men can do. They also pitch our tents, make and mend our clothing, keep us warm at night; and in fact there is no such thing as traveling any considerable distance, or for any length of time, in this country without their assistance.' 'Women,' said he again, 'though they do everything, are maintained at a trifling expense: for, as they always stand cook, the very licking of their fingers, in scarce times, is sufficient for their subsistence.'*

In 1769 the Hudson's Bay Company charged **Samuel Hearne** (British, 1745-1792) with the task of exploring the Barren Grounds of the central Canadian Arctic (a vast, treeless area between Hudson Bay and the Mackenzie River basin), in hopes of discovering sources of copper and a possible east-west passage through this northern region. After two failed attempts Hearne met a Chippewyan named Matonabbee, who agreed to act as guide if his numerous wives could accompany them. In Matonabbee's opinion, Hearne's earlier forays had failed because women had not been included in the parties. The third expedition (1770-1772) was arduous and succeeded, in Hearne's opinion, largely due to Matonabbee's leadership capabilities and the support of both the male and female members of his retinue.

STORES FOR GENERAL USE.

BEST FORM FOR MEMORANDA.

OUTFIT

It is impossible to include lists of outfit, in any reasonable space, that shall suit the various requirements of men engaged in expeditions of different magnitudes, who adopt different modes of locomotion, and who visit different countries and climates. I have therefore thought it best to describe only one outfit as a specimen, selecting for my example the desiderata for South Africa. The wants in that country are typical of those likely to be felt in every part of a large proportion of the region where rude travel is likely to be experienced, as in North Africa, in Australia, in Southern Siberia, and even in the prairies and pampas of North and South America. To make such an expedition effective all the articles included in the following lists may be considered as essential; I trust, on the other hand, that no article of real importance is omitted.

STORES FOR GENERAL USE.

☞ The quantities of stores for general use required for an expedition are to a great degree independent of the duration of the journey.

Small Stores, various :—	lbs.
One or two very small soft-steel axes; a small file to sharpen them; a few additional tools (see chapter on Timber); spare butcher's knives ..	8
A dozen awls for wood and for leather, two of them in handles; two gimlets; a dozen sail-needles; three palms; a ball of sewing-twine; bit of beeswax; sewing-needles, assorted; a ball of black and white thread; buttons; two tailors' thimbles (see chapter on Cord, String, and Thread)	3
Two penknives; small metal saw; bit of Turkey hone; large scissors; corkscrew	1½
Spring balances, from ¼ lb. to 5 lbs. and from 1 lb. to 50 lbs. (or else a hand steelyard)	1½
Fish-hooks of many sorts; cobbler's wax; black silk; gut; two or more fishing-lines and floats; a large ball of line; thin brass wire, for springes (see chapters on Fishing and Trapping)	2
Ball of wicks, for lamps; candle-mould (see chapter on Candles); a few corks; lump of sulphur; amadou (see chapter on Fire)	1½
Medicines (see chapter on Medicine); a scalpel; a blunt-pointed bistoury; and good forceps for thorns	1
A small iron, and an ironing-flannel; clothes-brush; bottle of Benzine or other scouring drops	3
Carried forward	21½

	lbs.
Brought forward	21½
Bullet-mould, not a heavy one; bit of iron plate for a ladle; gun-cleaning apparatus; turnscrews; nipple-wrench; bottle of fine oil; spare nipples; spare screw for cock (see chapter on Gun-Fittings)	2½
Two macintosh water-bags, shaped for the pack saddle, of one gallon each, with funnel-shaped necks, and having a wide mouth (empty) (see chapter on Water for Drinking)	2½
Composition for mending them, in two small bottles; and a spare piece of macintosh	0½
Spare leather, canvas, and webbing, for girths; rings and buckles	20
Two small patrol-tents, poles, and pegs (see chapter on Tents)	30
Small inflatable pontoon to hold one, or even two men (see chapter on Rafts and Boats)	10
Small bags for packing the various articles, independently of the saddle-bags	4
Macintosh sheeting overall, to keep the pack dry .. ..,	4
Total weight of various small stores	95

Heavy Stores, various :—	lbs.
Pack saddles, spare saddlery (see chapter on Harness); bags for packing Water-vessels (see chapter on Water for Drinking)	
Heavy ammunition for sporting purposes. (1 lb. weight gives 10 shots. Otherwise each armed man is supposed to carry a long double-barrelled rifle of very small bore, say of 70, and ammunition for these is allowed for below)	
Total weight of various heavy stores	

Stationery :—	lbs.
Two ledgers; a dozen note-books (see chapter on Memoranda and Log-Books); paper	9
Ink; pens; pencils; sealing-wax; gum	2½
Board to write upon	2
Books to read, say equal to six vols. the ordinary size of novels; and maps	7½
Bags and cases	3
Sketching-books, colours, and pencils	6
Total weight of stationery	30

Mapping :—	lbs.
Two sextants; horizon and roof; lantern; two pints of oil; azimuth compass; small aneroid; thermometers; tin-pot for boiling thermometers; watches (see chapter on Surveying Instruments)	18
Protractors; ruler; compasses; measuring-tape, &c.	3
Raper's Navigation; Nautical Almanac; Carr's Synopsis, published by Weale; small tables, and small almanacs; star maps	4
Bags and baskets, well wadded	6
Total weight of mapping materials	31

Natural History (for an occasional collector) :—	lbs.
Arsenical soap, 2 lbs.; camphor, ½ lb.; pepper, ½ lb.; bag of some powder to absorb blood, 2 lbs.; tow and cotton, about 10 lbs.; scalpel, forceps, scissors, &c., ½ lb.; sheet brass, stamped for labels, ½ lb.	16
Pill-boxes; cork; insect-boxes; pins; tin, for catching, and keeping, and killing, animals; nets for butterflies (say bags and all)	10
Geological hammers, lens, clinometer, &c.	4
Specimens. (I make no allowance for the weight of these, for they accumulate as stores are used up; and the total weight is seldom increased.)	
Total weight of Natural History materials (for an occasional collector)	30

☞ If meat and bread and the like have to be carried, a very large addition of weight must be made to this list, for the weight of a daily ration varies from 3 lbs., or even 4 lbs., to 2 lbs., according to the concentration of nutriment in the food that is used. Slaughter animals carry themselves; but the cattle watchers swell the list of those who have to be fed.

Heinrich Barth (German, 1821-65) joined British expeditions in Africa in 1849-55; his five-volume chronicle, *Travels and Discoveries in North and Central Africa*, is considered a classic work of geographic literature, with detailed information on the topography, history, cultures, and languages of the countries Barth visited. His own adventures make the reading that much more compelling. In Libya, for example, he climbed Mount Idinen, said by the Tuareg tribesmen to be a haunt of evil spirits. On the descent Barth became severely dehydrated and, wild with thirst, opened a vein and drank his own blood.

BEST FORM FOR MEMORANDA.

I have remarked that almost every traveler who is distinguished for the copiousness and accuracy of his journals, has written them in a remarkably small but distinct handwriting. Hard pencil marks (HHH pencils) on common paper, or on metallic paper, are very durable. Dr. Barth◆ wrote his numerous observations entirely in Indian ink. He kept a tiny saucer  in his pocket, rubbed with the ink; when he wanted to use it, he rubbed it up with his wetted fingertip, or resupplied it with fresh ink, and filled his pen and wrote. Captain Burton wrote very much in the dark, when lying awake at night; he used a board with prominent lines of wood, such as is adopted by the blind.

It is very important that what is written should be intelligible to a stranger after a long lapse of time. A traveler may die, and his uncompleted work perish with him; or he may return, and years will pass by, and suddenly some observations he had made will be called in question.

CLOTHING

There are such infinite varieties of dress, that I shall
only attempt a few general remarks and give a single
costume that a traveler of great experience had used
to his complete satisfaction. The military authorities
of different nations have long made it their study
to combine in the best manner the requirements of
handsome effect, of cheapness, and of serviceability
in all climates, but I fear their results will not greatly
help the traveler, who looks more to serviceability
than to anything else. Of late years, even Garibaldi
with his red-shirted volunteers, and Alpine men
with their simple outfit, have approached more
nearly to a traveler's ideal.

MATERIALS FOR CLOTHES.

Flannel. The importance of flannel next the skin
can hardly be overrated. It is now a matter of statistics, for, during the progress of expeditions, notes
have been made of the number of names of those
in them who had provided themselves with flannel
and of those who had not. The list of sick and dead
always included names from the latter list in a very
great proportion.

Cotton is preferable to flannel for a sedentary life,
in hot damp countries, or where flannel irritates the
skin. Persons who are resident in the tropics, and
dress in civilized costume, mostly wear cotton shirts.

Linen by universal consent is a dangerous dress
wherever there is a chance of much perspiration, for
it strikes cold upon the skin when it is wet. The terror of Swiss guides of the old school at a coup d'air

MATERIALS FOR CLOTHES.

EFFECT OF COLOR ON WARMTH OF CLOTHING.

WARMTH OF DIFFERENT MATERIALS.

WATERPROOF CLOTH.

ARTICLES OF DRESS.

WET CLOTHES, TO DRY.

TO KEEP CLOTHES FROM THE WET.

WASHING CLOTHES.

WASHING ONESELF.

☞ An outfit of sewing
materials consists of needles
and thread; scissors; tailor's
thimble; wax; canvas needles,
including the smaller sizes
which are identical with glove
needles and are used for
sewing leather; twine; a palm;
awls for cobbling, both straight
and curved; cobbler's wax;
and, possibly, bristles. The
needles and awls in use are
conveniently carried in some
kind of metal tube with wads of
cork at either end to preserve
their points.

Benjamin Thompson, a.k.a. **Count Rumford** (American, 1753-1814), aided the British during the American Revolution, and following the war spent the rest of his life in Britain and Europe. Possessed of an active scientific mind, during the war Thompson studied the explosive powers of gunpowder, which led to further studies in the area of thermodynamics. Among the heat-related inventions attributed to him are the double boiler, the drip coffee pot, thermal underwear, and the dessert called Baked Alaska. The Rumford fireplace, a tall, narrow style of firebox designed for maximum heat radiation, can be found in the rooms of Jefferson's Monticello, and is enjoying newfound popularity today due to its high efficiency.

on the mountain top, and of Italians at the chill of sundown, is largely due to their wearing linen shirts. Those who are dressed in flannel are far less sensitive to these influences.

Leather is the only safeguard against the stronger kinds of thorns. In pastoral and in hunting countries it is always easy to procure skins of a tough quality that have been neatly dressed by hand. Also it will be easy to find persons capable of sewing them together very neatly, after you have cut them out to the pattern of your old clothes.

Bark cloth is used in several parts of the world. It is simply a piece of some kind of peculiarly fibrous bark; in Unyoro, Sir S. Baker says, the natives use the bark of a species of fig tree. They soak it in water and then beat it with a mallet to get rid of all the harder parts, much as hemp is prepared. "In appearance it much resembles corduroy, and is the color of tanned leather: the finer qualities are peculiarly soft to the touch, as though of woven cotton."

EFFECT OF COLOR ON WARMTH OF CLOTHING.

Dark colors become hotter than light colors in the sunshine, but they are not hotter under any other circumstances. Consequently a person who aims at equable temperature should wear light colors. Light colors are far the best for sporting purposes, as they are usually much less conspicuous than black or rifle green.

WARMTH OF DIFFERENT MATERIALS.

The indefatigable Rumford◈ made an elaborate series of experiments on the conductivity of the substances used in clothing. The results are recorded in the following table:

Surrounded with—											Seconds.
Twisted silk	..	..	..	..	..	..	..	..	..	..	917
Fine lint..	..	..	..	..	..	..	..	..	..	..	1032
Cotton wool	..	..	..	..	..	..	..	..	..	..	1046
Sheep's wool	..	..	..	..	..	..	..	..	..	..	1118
Taffety	..	..	..	..	..	..	..	..	..	..	1169
Raw silk	..	..	..	..	..	..	..	..	..	..	1264
Beaver's fur	..	..	..	..	..	..	..	..	..	..	1296
Eider down	..	..	..	..	..	..	..	..	..	..	1305
Hare's fur	..	..	..	..	..	..	..	..	..	..	1312
Wood ashes	..	..	..	..	..	..	..	..	..	..	927
Charcoal	..	..	..	..	..	..	..	..	..	..	937
Lamp-black	..	..	..	..	..	..	..	..	..	..	1117

Among the substances here examined, hare's fur offered the greatest impediment to the transmission of the heat. The transmission of heat is powerfully influenced by the mechanical state of the body through which it passes. The raw and twisted silk of Rumford's table illustrate this. (Prof. Tyndall.)

WATERPROOF CLOTH.

Cloth is made partly waterproof by rubbing soap suds into it (on the wrong side) and working them well in, and, when dry, doing the same with a solution of alum; the soap is by this means decomposed and the oily part of it distributed among the fibers of the cloth.

ARTICLES OF DRESS.

Hats and caps. There is no perfect headdress; but I notice that old travelers in both hot and temperate countries have generally adopted a scanty "wide-awake." Mr. Oswell,◆ the South African sportsman and traveler, used for years, and strongly recommended to me, a brimless hat of fine Panama grass, which he had sewn as a lining to an ordinary

At the age of twenty-six **William Cotton Oswell** (British; 1818-1893) traveled to South Africa to recover from an illness he had contracted in India. He hunted and adventured throughout southern Africa, most notably with his close friend David Livingstone. In the introduction to Oswell's biography, Sir Francis Galton called him "the most dashing hunter and successful explorer of his time in southern Africa." He notes the irony of Livingstone's comparative fame when Oswell was, in fact, the experienced traveler who had invited Livingstone to accompany him on the famous initial journey to the African interior (which Oswell also financed). Galton surmises that Oswell's relative obscurity was due to "his invincible laziness as a writer."

☞ A muslin turban twisted into a rope and rolled round the hat is a common plan to keep the sun from the head and spine: it can also be used as a rope on an emergency.

☞ In cold dry weather, a pair of old soft kid gloves, with large woolen gloves drawn over them, is the warmest combination. To keep the hands warm in very severe weather, a small fur muff may be slung from the neck, in which the hands may rest till wanted.

wide-awake. I regret I have had no opportunity of trying this combination, but can easily believe that the touch of the cool, smooth grass to the wet brow would be more agreeable than that of any other material. I need hardly mention Pith hats, Indian topees, and English hunting cans as having severally many merits.

Coat. In nine cases out of ten, a strong but not too thick tweed coat is the best for rough work. In a very thorny country, a leather coat is almost essential. A blouse, cut short so as to clear the saddle, is neat, cool, and easy, whether as a riding or walking costume. Generally speaking, the traveler will chiefly spend his life in his shirtsleeves, and will only use his coat when he wants extra warmth.

To carry a coat. There are two ways. The first is to fold it small and strap it to the belt. If the coat be a light one it can be carried very neatly and comfortably in this way, lying in the small of the back. The second is the contrivance of a friend of mine, an eminent scholar and divine, who always employs it in his vacation rambles. It is to pass an ordinary strap, once round the middle of the coat and a second time round both the coat and the left arm just above the elbow, and then to buckle it. The coat hangs very comfortably in its place and does not hamper the movements of the left arm. It requires no further care, except that after a few minutes it will generally be found advisable to buckle the strap one hole tighter. A coat carried in this way will be found to attract no attention from passersby.

Trousers. If you are likely to have much riding, take extra leather or moleskin trousers, or tweed covered down the inside of the legs with leather, such as cavalry soldiers generally wear. Leather is a better protection than moleskin against thorns; but not so serviceable against wet: it will far outlast moleskin. There should be no hem to the legs of trousers, as it retains the wet.

Socks. The hotter the ground on which you have to walk, the thicker should be your socks. These should be of woolen, wherever you expect to have much walking; and plenty of them will be required.

Substitute for socks. For want of socks, pieces of linen may be used; and, when these are properly put on, they are said to be even better than socks. They should be a foot square, be made of soft worn linen, be washed once a day, and be smeared with tallow. They can be put on so dexterously as to stand several hours' marching without making a single wrinkle, and are much used by soldiers in Germany. To put them on, the naked foot is placed crosswise; the corners on the right and on the left are then folded over, then the corner which lies in front of the toes. Now the art consists in so drawing up these ends, that the foot can be placed in the shoe or boot without any wrinkles appearing in the bandage. One wrinkle is sure to make a blister, and therefore persons who have to use them should practice frequently how to put them on. Socks similar to these, but made of thick blanket, and called "blanket wrappers," are in use at Hudson's Bay instead of shoes.

☞ Persons who travel, even with the smallest quantity of luggage, would do wisely to take a thick dressing gown. It is a relief to put it on in the evening, and is a warm extra dress for sleeping in. It is eminently useful, comfortable and durable.

☞ When you have occasion to tuck up your shirt-sleeves, recollect that the way of doing so is not to begin by turning the cuffs inside out, but outside in—the sleeves must be rolled up inwards, towards the arm, and not the reverse way. In the one case, the sleeves will remain tucked up for hours without being touched; in the other, they become loose every five minutes.

☞ Haybands wound round
the feet are a common makeshift by soldiers who are cut off
from their supplies.

☞ It takes some months to
harden the feet sufficiently to
be able to walk without shoes
at all.

☞ Slippers are great luxuries
to footsore men. They should
of course be of soft material,
but the soles should not be too
thin or they will be too cold for
comfort in camp life.

Boots. Boots of tanned leather such as civilized
people wear are incomparably better for hard
usage, especially in wet countries, than those of
hand-dressed skins. If traveling in a hot, dry country, grease plentifully both your shoes and all other
leather. "La graisse est la conservation du cuir," as
I recollect a Chamonix guide enunciating with
profound emphasis. The soles of plaited cord used in
parts of the Pyrenees are durable and excellent for
clambering over smooth rock. They have a far better
hold upon it than any other sole of which I have
knowledge. Sandals are better than nothing at all.
So are cloths wound round the feet and ankles and
tied there; the peasants of the remarkable hilly place
where I am writing these lines, namely Amalfi, use
them much. They are an untidy chaussure, but never
seem to require to be tied afresh. In the old days of
Rome this sort of footgear was common.

Leggings. Macintosh leggings to go over the
trousers are a great comfort in heavy showers, especially when riding.

Gaiters. If the country be full of briars and
thorns, the insteps suffer cruelly when riding
through bushes. It is easy to make gaiters either with
buttons or buckles. A strip of wood is wanted, either
behind or else on each side of them, to keep them
from slipping down to the ankle.

Poncho. A poncho is useful, for it is a sheet as
well as a cloak; being simply a blanket with a slit in
the middle to admit the wearer's head. A sheet of
strong calico, saturated with oil, makes a waterproof
poncho.

WET CLOTHES, TO DRY.

To dry clothes it is a very convenient plan to make a dome-shaped framework of twigs over a smoldering fire, by bending each twig or wand into a half-circle and planting both ends of it in the ground, one on each side of the fire. The wet clothes are laid on this framework, and receive the full benefit of the heat. Their steam passes readily upwards.

TO KEEP CLOTHES FROM THE WET.

Mr. Parkyns says,

I may as well tell, also, how we managed to keep our clothes dry when traveling in the rain: this was rather an important consideration, seeing that each man's wardrobe consisted of what he carried on his back. Our method was at once effective and simple: if halting, we took off our clothes and sat on them; if riding, they were placed under the leathern shabraque of the mule's saddle, or under any article of similar material, bed or bag, that lay on the camel's pack. A good shower-bath did none of us any harm; and as soon as the rain was over, and the moisture on our skins had evaporated, we had our garments as warm, dry, and comfortable, as if they had been before a fire. In populous districts, we kept on our drawers, or supplied their place with a piece of rag, or a skin; and then, when the rain was over, we wrapped ourselves up in our 'quarry,' and taking off the wetted articles, hung them over the animal's cruppers to dry.

Another traveler writes: "The only means we had of preserving our sole suit of clothes dry from the drenching showers of rain, was by taking them off and stuffing them into the hollow of a tree, which, in the darkness of the night, we could do with propriety."

Mr. Palliser's boatmen at Chagre took each a small piece of cloth, under which they laid their clothes every time that they stripped in expectation of a coming storm.

A good shower-bath did none of us any harm

By the end of his career with the British Royal Navy, **William Bligh** (British, 1754-1817) had attained the station of vice-admiral. Still, we persist in knowing him as Captain Bligh, leader of the ill-fated 1787 voyage to Tahiti to collect breadfruit trees for delivery to the Caribbean as a potential food crop for slaves. Bligh first went to sea as a ship's boy just shy of his eighth birthday, and for close to fifty years he held positions of increasing responsibility aboard many vessels—but perhaps none as challenging as his command of the 23-foot launch set adrift by the mutineers of the *Bounty*, in which he navigated 3,618 nautical miles to Timor in 41 days. His gravestone in an English churchyard is decorated with a breadfruit.

Dipping clothes wetted with rain, in seawater. Captain Bligh,◈ who was turned adrift in an open boat after the mutiny of the *Bounty*, writes thus about his experience:

> *With respect to the preservation of our health, during a course of 16 days of heavy and almost continual rain, I would recommend to every one in a similar situation the method we practiced, which is to dip their clothes in the salt water and wring them out as often as they become filled with rain: it was the only resource we had, and I believe was of the greatest service to us, for it felt more like a change of dry clothes than could well be imagined. We had occasion to do this so often, that at length our clothes were wrung to pieces; for except the few days we passed on the coast of New Holland, we were continually wet, either with rain or sea.*

WASHING CLOTHES.

The lye of ashes and the gall of animals are the readiest substitutes for soap. The sailor's recipe for washing clothes is well known, but it is too dirty to describe. Bran, and the meal of many seeds, is good for scouring: also some earths, like fuller's-earth. Many countries possess plants that will make a lather with water. Dr. Rae◈ says that in a very cold climate, when fire, water, and the means of drying are scarce, it will be found that rubbing and beating in snow cleanses all clothing remarkably well, particularly woolens. When preparing for a regular day's washing, it is a good plan to boil an abundance of ashes in water, strain off the lye, adding the gall of any animal you may have killed, and let the clothes soak in it. Next morning, take them to the waterside and wash and beat them with a flat piece of wood, or lay them on a broad stone and knead and wring them with the hands.

WASHING ONESELF.

Warmth of dirt. There is no denying the fact, though it be not agreeable to confess it, that dirt and grease are great protectors of the skin against inclement weather, and that therefore the leader of a party should not be too exacting about the appearance of his less warmly-clad followers. There must be a balance between the activity of the skin and the calls upon it; and where the exposure is greater, there must the pores be more defended. In Europe, we pass our lives in a strangely artificial state, our whole body swathed in many folds of dress, excepting the hands and face—the first of which are frequently gloved. We can afford to wash, but naked men cannot.

Best times for washing. The most convenient time for a traveler to make his toilet, in rough travel, is after the early morning's ride, a bath being now and then taken in the afternoon. It is trying work to wash in ice-cold water, in the dark and blowing morning; besides which, when the sun rises up, its scorching heat tells severely on a face that has been washed.

Toilet made overnight. During the harassing duties of active warfare, officers who aim at appearing in a decorous dress, in whatever emergency their presence may be required, make their toilet overnight before going to sleep.

Dr. John Rae (British, 1813-1893), a Scottish surgeon who joined the Hudson's Bay Company at the age of twenty, spent much of the next thirty years exploring the Canadian Arctic. Rae was a willing student of the native peoples he encountered (an attitude rare at the time); he learned critical survival skills from the Cree and Inuit—how to make clothing from furs, build igloos, and prevent snow blindness, for example—that enabled him to explore and map close to 2,000 miles of terrain. He was the foremost Arctic authority of his time, and the skills he acquired were applied by subsequent explorers, such as Roald Amundsen, to stay alive in the harshest conditions.

☞ Where water has to be economized, by far the best way of using it is after the Mohammedan fashion. An attendant pours a slender stream from a jug, which the man who washes himself receives in his hands and distributes over his person.

ESTIMATIONS OF LOADS.

HORSES.

MULES.

ASSES.

OXEN.

ELEPHANTS..

DOGS.

GOATS AND SHEEP.

MANAGEMENT OF CATTLE, GENERALLY.

WAGONS.

SLEDGES.

SADDLES FOR RIDING.

NORTH AMERICAN TRAVAIL.

PALANQUINS.

BEASTS OF BURDEN

In fitting out a caravan, as few different kinds of animals should be taken as possible, or they will split into separate herds and require many men to look after them. The dispositions of the animals that compose a caravan affect, in no small degree, the pleasure of traveling with it. Now, it is to be noticed that men attach themselves to horses and asses, and in a lesser degree to mules and oxen, but they rarely make friends of camels.

ESTIMATIONS OF LOADS.

The net weights that different animals carry in trying, long-continued journeys—through stages uncertain in length, sometimes leading to good pasture, sometimes to bad—must not be reckoned higher than the following; and an animal draws about twenty-two times as much net weight as he carries.

> *An ass will not usually*
> *carry more than about (net wt.)* .... *65 lbs.*
> *A small mule* .... *90 lbs.*
> *A horse* .... *100 lbs.*
> *An ox of an average breed* .... *120 lbs.*
> *A camel (which rarely can be*
> *used by an explorer)* .... *300 lbs.*
> *An elephant* .... *500 lbs.*

Carriages. An animal—camels always excepted—draws upon wheels in a wild country about two and a half times the weight he can carry.

Travails. Dogs will draw a travail of 60 lbs. for a distance of 15 miles a day upon hard level country.

In level countries—where there is grain, and where

☞ It is very inconvenient to take more than six pack-animals in a caravan that has to pass over broken country, for so much time is lost by the whole party in readjusting the packs of each member of it, whenever one gets loose, that its progress is seriously retarded.

the road is known and a regularity in the day's work can be ensured—the weights that may be carried are fully double those listed. Captain Burton's◆ donkeys, in East Africa, carried immense weights.

Theory of Loads and Distances. How should we load men or animals of transport, and how should we urge them, in order to obtain the largest amount of effective labor? If they carry a mere feather-weight, they may make long days' journeys; but their value, as animals of transport, is almost nothing. Again, on the other hand, if we load them with an excessive weight, they will soon come to a standstill; and in this case, as in the first, their value as beasts of transport is almost nil. What, then, is that moderate load by which we shall obtain the largest amount of "useful effect"?

This is a problem which many of the ablest engineers and philosophers have endeavored to solve; and the formulae—partly based on theory and partly on experiment—which were used by Euler, are generally accepted as a fair approximation. They are very simple, and peculiarly interesting on account of their wide applicability. They are equally true for men, animals, or machines; and are wholly independent of the way in which the power is applied: whether, for instance, a man carries his burden, or draws it, or rows or punts it in a boat, or winds it up with a crank or treadmill.

An animal gets through most work in the day if he carries four-ninths of the greatest load he could just stagger under; in which case he will be able to travel a third of the distance he could walk if he carried no load at all. As an example: Suppose a man

Captain **Richard Francis Burton** (British, 1821-90), the famous adventurer, was an accomplished explorer, writer, translator, linguist, and ethnologist. He served in the army in India; for the Royal Geographic Society he explored portions of Africa; and he traveled widely in Asia and Arabia. He is perhaps best known for his journey with John Hanning Speke in search of the source of the Nile River. Burton wrote or translated more than thirty books, including the first translation of *The Arabian Nights,* considered pornographic at the time.

John Solomon Rarey
(American, 1827-66) gained
international renown for his
ability to tame the wildest
and most malevolent horses
in just hours. He tamed his
first horse at age twelve; as
an adult he traveled widely,
demonstrating his technique
for awed onlookers, including
the queen of England. It once
took him only four hours
to train a wild zebra so that
anyone could handle or ride it.
Rarey's technique was based
upon kindness and respect for
the animal, so different from
the prevailing belief in physical
force for breaking a horse.
Rarey is now called the original
horse whisperer.

is able to walk 10 miles a day, with a load of 130 lbs., and 33 miles a day when he carries nothing. Then the burden under which he would be brought to a standstill would be about 267½, and the best load for him would be 119 lbs., which he would be able to carry 11 miles a day.

HORSES.

The mode of taking wild horses is by throwing the lasso, whilst pursuing them at full speed, and dropping a noose over their necks, by which their speed is soon checked, and they are choked down.

Mr. Rarey's◈ sixpenny book tells all that can be told on the subject of horse breaking; but far more lies in the skill and horse knowledge of the operator, than in the mere theory. His way of mastering a vicious 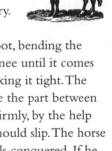 horse is by taking up one forefoot, bending the knee, slipping a loop over the knee until it comes to the pastern joint, and then fixing it tight. The loop must be caused to embrace the part between the hoof and the pastern joint firmly, by the help of a strap of some kind, lest it should slip. The horse is now on three legs, and he feels conquered. If he gets very mad, wait leisurely till he becomes quiet, then caress him, and let the leg down and allow him to rest; then repeat the process. If the horse kicks in harness, drive him slowly on three legs.

Picketing. Horses are often tied to the wheels, &tc., of the wagon. When you wish to picket horses in the middle of a sandy plain, dig a hole 2 or 3 feet deep, and tying your rope to a faggot of sticks or brushwood, or even to a bag filled with sand, bury this in it.

Addenda. In climbing a steep hill hang on to the tail of your horse as you walk behind him. Horses are easily driven in file by securing the halter of each horse to the tail of the one before him.

MULES.

Mules require men who know their habits; they are powerful beasts, and can only be mastered with skill and address. They have odd secret ways, strange fancies, and lurking vice. When they stray, they go immense distances and it is almost beyond the power of a man on foot to tend them in a wild country; he can neither overtake them easily, nor, when overtaken, catch them. The female is, in most breeds, much the more docile. They suffer from African distemper, but in a less degree than horses.

The following descriptions of mule caravans are exceedingly graphic and instructive:

> The madrina (or godmother) is a most important personage. She is an old steady mare, with a little bell round her neck, and wheresoever she goes the mules, like good children, follow her. If several large troops are turned into one field to graze in the morning, the muleteer has only to lead the madrinas a little apart and tinkle their bells, and, although there may be 200 or 300 mules together, each immediately knows its own bell, and separates itself from the rest. The affection of these animals for their madrina saves infinite trouble. It is nearly impossible to lose an old mule: for, if detained several hours by force, she will, by the power of smell, like a dog, track out her companions, or rather the madrina; for, according to the muleteer, she is the chief object of affection. The feeling, however, is not of an individual nature; for I believe I am right in saying that any animal with a bell will serve as a madrina. (Charles Darwin)

☞ Mungo Park tells how he clutched his horse's muzzle with both hands to prevent his neighing, when he was in concealment and horsemen were passing near.

Mules have odd secret ways, strange fancies, and lurking vice

ASSES.

Notwithstanding his inveterate obstinacy, the ass is an excellent and sober little beast, far too much despised by us. He is not only the most enduring, but also one of the quickest walkers among cattle, being usually promoted to the leadership of a caravan. He is nearly equal to the camel in enduring thirst, and thrives on the poorest pasture, suffers from few diseases, and is unscathed by African distemper. The long desert roads and pilgrim tracts of North Africa are largely traveled over by means of asses.

Not to bray. Messrs. Hue◆ and Gabet, who were distracted by the continual braying of one of their asses throughout the night, appealed to their muleteer: he put a speedy close to the nuisance by what appears to be a customary contrivance in China, viz., by lashing a heavy stone to the beast's tail. It appears that when an ass wants to bray he elevates his tail, and, if his tail be weighted down, he has not the heart to bray. In hostile neighborhoods, where silence and concealment are sought, it might be well to adopt this rather absurd treatment.

OXEN.

Though oxen are coarse, gross, and phlegmatic beasts, they have these merits: they are eminently gregarious, and they ruminate their food. The consequence is, first, that one, two, or more are very seldom missing out of a drove; and, secondly, that they pick up what they require in a much shorter time than horses, mules, &c., who have to chew as

Father Evariste R. Hue (French, 1813-60), a Catholic missionary, traveled overland from China to Tibet in 1844-46 with Father Joseph Gabet on an assignment to study the tribal customs of nomadic Mongols to determine how best to evangelize them. Hue was the author of *Travels in Tartary, Thibet and China*, published in eight languages.

they eat. Oxen require less tending than any other beasts of burden.

To train a pack ox. An ox of any age, however wild he may be, can be broken in, in three or four days, so as to carry a pack of about 70 lbs.; though it is true that he will frequently kick it off during the journey and give excessive trouble. It would be scarcely possible to drive more than three of these newly-taught oxen at a time, on account of the frequent delays caused by the unruliness of one or other of them.

To train an ox to carry a rider. It takes a very long time to train an ox to carry a riding saddle well and steadily; indeed, very few oxen can be taught to go wherever they may be guided by the rider; they are of so gregarious a nature that, for the most part, they will not move a step without companions. Hence, those oxen only are thought worth breaking in which are observed to take the part of leaders of the drove when pasturing, and which are therefore supposed to have some independence of disposition.

After being mounted a very few times, the ox goes pretty steadily; but it is long before he learns to carry a rider with ease to himself. In riding, it must be recollected that the temper of an ox is far less quick, though his sensations may be as acute as those of a horse; thus, he does not start forwards on receiving a cut with the whip, even though he shrink with the pain; but he thinks about it, shakes his head, waits a while, and then breaks gradually into a faster pace.

☞ Much depends on the natural aptitude of the animal in estimating the time required for making a steady pack ox; some will carry a good weight and go steadily after only a fortnight's travel; some will never learn. But in all cases they prove unruly at the beginning of a journey.

☞ To make ride oxen quiet and tame, scratch their backs and tails—they dearly love it—and hold salt in your hands for them to lick. They soon learn their names, and come to be caressed when called.

☞ The first time of mounting an ox to break him in is a work of almost certain mischance: for the long horns of the ox will often reach the rider, however far back he may sit, and the animal kicks and bucks in a way that severely tries the best of seats. All riding oxen's horns should have the tips sawn off.

☞ Camels are only fit for
a few countries, and require
practiced attendants; thorns
and rocks lame them, hills sadly
impede them, and a wet slippery
soil entirely stops them.

ELEPHANTS.

They are expensive and delicate, but excellent beasts of burden in rainy tropical countries.
The traveler should make friends with the one he
regularly rides by giving it a piece of sugar cane or
banana before mounting. A sore back is a certain
obstacle to a continuance of travel; there is no
remedy for it but rest. The average burden, furniture
included, but excluding the driver, is 500 lbs., and
the full average day's journey 15 miles.

DOGS.

For Arctic travel, dogs are used in journeys after
they are three years old; each dog requires eight
or ten herrings per day, or an equivalent to them.
A sledge of 12 dogs carries 900 lbs.; it travels on
smooth ice 7 or 8 miles an hour; and in 36 days,
22 sledges and 240 dogs traveled 800 miles—1210
versts. (Admiral Wrangel.◈)

GOATS AND SHEEP.

When the Messrs. Schlagintweit◆ were encamped at vast heights, among the snows of the
Himalaya, they always found it practicable to
drive sheep to their stations. Goats are much more
troublesome to drive than sheep, neither are they
such enduring walkers, nor do they give as much
meat; but their skins are of such great use to furnish
strong leather, that it is seldom convenient to make
up a caravan without them.

She-goats give some milk, even when traveling
fast, and in dry countries; but a ewe-sheep is not
worth milking under those circumstances, as her
yield is a mere nothing. Goats are very mischie-

An admiral of the Russian navy
and a founder of the Russian
Geographic Society, **Baron
Ferdinand von Wrangel**
(Russian, 1796-1870) explored
polar regions of Siberia, the
Arctic Ocean, and Alaska. Nine
geographic features are named
for him, including two islands,
a cape, a channel, a volcano,
and a group of mountains.

vous—they make their way out of all enclosures, and trespass everywhere. They butt at whatever is bright or new, or strange to them; and would drive to distraction an observer who employed astronomical instruments on stands.

MANAGEMENT OF CATTLE GENERALLY.

To make an animal rise when he throws himself on the ground with his pack, and will not get up, it is not of much use to flog him; twisting or biting his tail is the usual way, or making a blaze with grass and a few sticks under his nostrils. The stubbornness of a half-broken ox is sometimes beyond conception.

Brands and cattle marks. In buying oxen out of the herds of pastoral people, it is very difficult to remember each animal so as to recognize it again if it strays back to its former home; it requires quite a peculiar talent to do so. Therefore it is advisable that the traveler's cattle should be marked or branded. A trader in Namaqua Land took red paint, and tied a brush onto a long stick; with this he made a daub on the hind quarters of the freshly-bought and half-wild cattle as they pushed through the door of his kraal. It naturally excites great ridicule among natives to paint an ox that he may be known again; but, for all that, I think the trader's plan well worth adopting.

Chaff, to cut. Cattle will eat many sorts of herbage, as reeds and gorse, if cut small, but will not touch them if uncut. Tie a sickle against a tree with its blade projecting; then, standing in front of the blade, hold a handful of reeds across it with both hands, one hand on either side of the blade; pull

Over the course of fifty-odd years, beginning in 1846, various combinations of the five **Schlagintweit** brothers (German; **Hermann,** 1826-82; **Adolf,** 1829-57; **Eduard,** 1831-66; **Robert,** 1833-85; and **Emil,** 1835-1904), conducted studies of the physical geography, natural science, and ethnography of Europe, central Asia, northern Africa, and North America.

☞ A good way of marking a sheep's ear is to cut a wad out of the middle of it with a gunpunch, but it will sometimes tear this hole into a slit by scratching with its foot.

it towards you, and the reeds will be cut through; drop the cut end, seize the bundle afresh, and repeat the process. In this way, after a little practice, chaff is cut with great ease and quickness. A broken sickle does as well as a whole one, and a knife may be used, but the curve of its edge is ill-adapted for the work.

Pulling cattle out of holes. The bight of a cord, or of some substitute for one, may be thrown over a horse's head, and he can be dragged out by a team of cattle with but very little danger to his neck. A crupper under his tail, or a thong as a breeching may be used. In Canada and the United States, a noose of rope is often run round the horse's neck and hauled tight—thus temporarily choking the animal and making him still; he is then pulled as quickly as possible out of the hole, and no time is lost in slackening the rope.

WAGONS.

A traveler's wagon should be of the simplest possible construction, and not too heavy. The Cape wagons, or, at all events, those of a few years back, undoubtedly shared the ponderousness of all Dutch workmanship. Weight is required only when crash-

☞ In countries where they can be used without danger, cattle bells should always be taken; it adds greatly to the cheerfulness and gregarious-ness of the animals—mules positively require them. Hard wood is sonorous enough for bells.

ing through a bushy country, where a wagon must break down all before it; in every other case it is objectionable. It is a saving of labor to have one large wagon, rather than two small ones, because a driver and a leader are thereby spared.

SLEDGES.

When carrying wood or stones, and doing other heavy work, a traveler should spare his wagon and use a sledge. This is made by cutting down a forked tree, lopping off its branches, and shaping it a little with an axe. If necessary, a few bars may be fixed

across the fork so as to make a stage. Great distances may be traversed by one of these rude affairs if the country is not very stony. Should it capsize, no great harm is done; and if it breaks down, or is found to have been badly made, an hour's labor will suffice to construct another. Sledges are very useful where there is an abundance of horse or ox power but no wagon or packing gear.

NORTH AMERICAN TRAVAIL.

In a North American Indian horse "travail," the crossing of the poles (they are the poles of the wigwams) usually rests on a rough pack saddle or pad, which a breast strap keeps from slipping backwards. In a dog travail the cross of the poles rests on the back of the neck, and is kept in place by a breast or rather a neck strap; the poles are wrapped with pieces of buffalo robe where they press against the dog.

Thomas Wright Blakiston
(English, 1832-1891) explored
in western Canada and China
before becoming a prominent
naturalist of Japan, where
he collected a specimen of
a tremendous owl—with a
wingspan reaching 6 feet—that
was later named after him.
Blakiston was the first person
to notice that animals in
Hokkaido, Japan's northern
island, were related to northern Asian species, whereas
those on Honshu to the south
were related to those from
southern Asia. The Tsugaru
Strait between the two islands
was therefore established as a
major zoogeographical bound-
ary and became known as the
Blakiston Line.

*Half a dozen
palanquins in file
would make a
pretty caravan*

Captain Blakiston◆—a very accurate authority—considers that a horse will travel 30 miles in
the day, dragging on the travail a weight of about
200 lbs., including a child, whose mother sits on the
horse's back; and that a dog, the size of an average
retriever, will draw about 80 lbs. for the same distance. (N.B. The North American plains are perfectly
level.)

PALANQUINS.

Palanquins, carried like sedan chairs, between
two animals—one going before the other in
shafts—are in use in various countries; but I am
not aware that explorers have ever properly tried
them. Their advantage would lie in combining the
convenience of a cart with much of the independence of pack horses. For whatever is lashed on a
pack saddle must be securely tied up; it is therefore
severely compressed, and cannot be taken out en
route. But with a cart or a palanquin there is no
such inconvenience: things may be quickly thrown
into them or taken out; pockets and drawers may
be fitted up; and the palanquin would afford some
shelter in rain. Half a dozen palanquins in file would
make a pretty, and, I should think, a manageable and
effective caravan.

CLIMBING AND MOUNTAINEERING

CLIMBING TREES.

Colonel Jackson,◈ in his book, *How to Observe (sic)*, gives the following directions for climbing palms and other trees that have very rough barks:

> Take a strip of linen, or two towels or strong handkerchiefs tied together, and form a loop at each end, for the feet to pass tightly into without going through; or, for want of such material, make a rope of grass or straw in the same way. The length should embrace a little more than half of the diameter of the trunk to be climbed. Now, being at the foot of the tree, fix the feet well into the loops, and opening the legs a little, embrace the tree as high up as you can. Raise your legs, and, pressing the cord against the tree with your feet, stand, as it were, in your stirrups, and raise your body and arms higher; hold fast again by the arms, open the legs, and raise them a stage higher, and so on to the top. The descent is effected in the same way, reversing, of course, the order of the movements. The ruggedness of the bark, and the weight of the body pressing diagonally across the trunk of the tree, prevent the rope from slipping. Anything, provided it be strong enough, is better than a round rope, which does not hold so fast.

A loop or hoop embracing the body of the climber and the tree is a helpful addition. Large nails carried in a bag slung round the waist, to be driven into the bare trunk of the tree, will facilitate its ascent. Gimlets may be used for the same purpose. High walls can be climbed by help of this description: a weight attached to one end of a rope, being first thrown over the wall, and the climber assisting himself by holding on to the other end. Trees of soft wood are climbed by cutting notches 2 feet apart on alternate sides. Also by driving in bamboo pegs,

CLIMBING TREES.

LOWERING OFF ROCK FACES.

KNOTS.

SNOW MOUNTAINS.

Colonel Julian Jackson, a secretary of New Zealand's Royal Society of Fellows, was the author of *What to Observe: Or, The Traveler's Remembrancer* (1841). At a time when travelers considered it their duty to return home with useful data gathered during their movements through foreign lands, Jackson's book prepared them to be assid-uous in developing "a true knowledge of the Earth, and of the Laws, Religion, Manners, and customs of Mankind."

sloping alternately to left or to right; these pegs correspond to the "rungs" of a ladder.

Ladders. A notched pole or a knotted rope makes a ladder. We hear of people who have tied sheets together to let themselves down high walls, when making an escape. The best·way of making a long rope from sheets is to cut them into strips of about 6 inches broad, and with these to twist a two-stranded rope, or else to plait a three-stranded one.

LOWERING OFF ROCK FACES.

Descending cliffs with ropes is an art which naturalists and others have occasion to practice. It has been reduced to a system by the inhabitants of some rocky coasts in the Northern seas, where innumerable seabirds go for the breeding season, and whose ledges and crevices are crammed with nests full of large eggs, about the end of May and the beginning of June. They are no despicable prize to a hungry native. I am indebted to a most devoted rock climber, the late Mr. Woolley, for the following facts. It appears that the whole population are rock climbers in the following places: St. Kilda, in the Hebrides; Foula Island, in Shetland; the Faroe Islands generally; and in the Westmaroer Islands off Iceland. Flamborough Head used to be a famous place for this accomplishment, but the birds have become far less numerous; they have been destroyed very wantonly with shot.

In descending a cliff, two ropes are used; one a supple well-made, many-stranded inch rope to which the climber is attached, and by which he is let down; the other is a much thinner cord, left to

☞ In St. Kilda, leather ropes are used: they last a lifetime, and are a dowry for a daughter.

☞ In the Faroes, they tar the ropes excessively; they are absolutely polished with tar.

☞ Turf and solid rock are much the best substances for the rope to run over.

dangle over the cliff, and made fast to some stone or stake above. The use of the second rope is for the climber to haul upon when he wishes to be pulled up. By resting a large part of his weight upon it, he makes the task of pulling him up much more easy. He can also convey signals by jerking it.

A usual rock climbing arrangement is shown in the sketch. One man with a post behind him, as in fig. 1, or two men, as in fig. 2, are entrusted with the letting down of a comrade to the depth of 100 or even 150 feet. They pass the rope either under their thighs or along their sides, as shown in the figures. The climber is attached to the rope, as shown in fig. 2. The band on which he sits is of worsted. A beginner ought to be attached far more securely to the rope.

It is nervous work going over the edge of a cliff for the first time; however, the sensation does not include giddiness. Once in the air, and when

It is nervous work going over the edge of a cliff for the first time; however, the sensation does not include giddiness

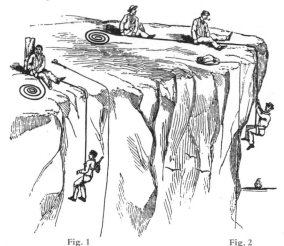

Fig. 1   Fig. 2

☞ It is convenient, but not necessary, to have a well-greased leather sheath, a tube of 18 inches in length, through which the rope runs, as shown in both figures. It lies over the edges of the cliff, and the friction of the rock keeps it steadily in its place.

confidence is acquired, the occupation is very exhilarating. The power of locomotion is marvelous: a slight push with the foot, or a thrust with a stick, will swing the climber 20 feet to a side. Few rocks are so precipitous but that a climber can generally make some use of his hands and feet, enough to cling to the rock when he wishes, and to clamber about its face.

Precautions. There are three safety measures to be borne in mind.

1. As you go down, test every stone carefully. If the movement of the rope displaces any one of them, after you have been let down below it, it is nearly sure to fall upon your head, because you will be vertically beneath it. Some climbers use a kind of helmet as a shield against these very dangerous accidents.

2. Take care that the rope does not become jammed in a cleft, or you will be helplessly suspended in mid-air.

3. Keep the rope pretty tight when you are clambering about the ledges: else, if you slip, the jerk may break the rope, or cause an overpowering strain upon the men who are holding it above.

☞ The wind is seldom felt by a person touching the face of a precipice: it may blow a gale above, but the air will be comparatively quiet upon its face; and therefore there is no danger of a chance gush dashing the climber against the rocks.

KNOTS.

I give the following extracts from the *Report of a Committee Appointed by the Alpine Club in 1864, on Ropes, Axes, and Alpenstocks:*

1. No knot, which is not absolutely necessary, ought to be allowed to remain on the rope.

2. The tighter and harder a knot becomes, the worse it is.

3. The more loose and open a knot is made, the

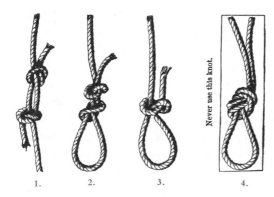

Never use this knot.

1.   2.   3.   4.

better it is—and we append diagrams of those knots which we found by experiment weaken the rope least.

For Alpine ropes, only three sorts of knots are ever required, and we suggest one of each kind:

No. 1 is for the purpose of joining two ends.

No. 2 is for the purpose of making a loop at one end.

No. 3 is for the purpose of making a loop in the middle when the ends are fastened.

No. *4* is a knot, of which we give a diagram in order that no one may imitate it. It is one of those which most weaken the rope. The only one which seemed to be equally injurious is the common single knot, of which no diagram is necessary.

SNOW MOUNTAINS.

The real dangers of the high Alps may be reduced to three:

1. Yielding of snow bridges over crevices.

2. Slipping on slopes of ice.

3. The fall of ice, or rocks, from above.

☞ Always face difficult places; if you slip, let your first effort be to turn upon your stomach, for in every other position you are helpless. A mountaineer, when he meets with a formidable obstacle, does not hold on the rock by means of his feet and his hands only, but he clings to it like a caterpillar, with every part of his body that can come simultaneously into contact with its roughened surface.

Absolute security from the first is obtainable by tying the party together at intervals to a rope. If there be only two in company, they should be tied together at eight or ten paces apart. Against the second danger, the rope is usually effective, though frightful accidents have occurred by the fall of one man, dragging along with him the whole chain of his companions. Against the third danger there is no resource but circumspection. Ice falls chiefly in the heat of the day; it is from limestone cliffs that the falling rocks are nearly always detached. When climbing ice of the most moderate slope, nailed boots are an absolute necessity; and for steep slopes of ice, the ice axe is equally essential.

Alpine outfit consists of ropes, ice axe or alpenstock (there must be at least one ice axe in the party), nailed boots, colored spectacles, veil or else a linen mask, muffettees, and gaiters.

Boots. Several nails are sure to be knocked out after each hard day's work therefore a reserve supply is necessary in lands where none other are to be found. No makeshift contrivance, so far as I am aware, will replace the iron last used by shoemakers when they hammer nails into the boot. There is a well-known contrivance of screws with jagged heads, for screwing into boots when a little ice has to be crossed. They do excellently for occasional purposes, but not for regular ice work, as they are easily torn out. Crampons are soles of leather with spikes; they are tied over the shoes, but neither English mountaineers nor modern guides ever employ them; nailed boots are better.

Snow spectacles. The Eskimo, who have no colored glass, or any equivalent for it, cut a piece of soft wood to the curvature of the face; it is about 2 inches thick and extends horizontally quite across both eyes, resting on the nose, a notch being cut in the wood to answer the purpose of the bridge of a pair of spectacles. It is tied behind the ears, and, so far as I have now described it, would exclude every ray of light from the eyes. Next, a long narrow slit, of the thickness of a thin sawcut, is made along its middle almost from end to end. Through this slit the wearer can see very fairly. As it is narrower than the diameter of the pupil of his eye, the light that reaches his retina is much diminished in quantity. Crepe or gauze is a substitute for colored glass.

Mask. This is merely a pocket handkerchief with strings to tie it over the face; eyeholes are cut in it, also a hole for the nose, over which a protecting triangular piece of linen is thrown, and another hole opposite the mouth to breathe through; it is drawn below the chin so as to tie firmly in place. The mask prevents the face from being cut to pieces by the cold dry winds, and blistered by the powerful rays of the sun reverberated from the snow.

LEARNING TO SWIM.

LANDING THROUGH
BREAKERS.

FLOATS.

SWIMMING WITH HORSES.

WATER SPECTACLES.

☞ People swim much more slowly than is commonly supposed. In races between first-rate swimmers, for distances of 300 yards and upwards, the average pace of two miles an hour is barely, if at all, exceeded.

SWIMMING

LEARNING TO SWIM.

A good way of teaching a person to swim is a modification of that adopted at Eton. The teacher may sit in a punt or on a rock, with a stout stick of 6 or 10 feet in length, at the end of which is a cord of 4 feet or so, with loops. The learner puts himself into the loops and the teacher plays him, as a fisherman would play a fish, in water that is well out of his depth; he gives him just enough support to keep him from drowning. After six or a dozen lessons, many boys require no support at all, but swim about with the rope dangling slack about them. When a boy does this, he can be left to shift for himself.

The art of swimming far is acquired, like the art of running far, by a determination to go on, without resting a moment, until utterly unable to make a stroke further, and then to stop altogether. Each succeeding day, the distance traveled is marvelously increased, until the natural limit of the man's powers is attained.

To support those who cannot swim. If a person cannot swim a stroke, he should be buoyed up with floats under his arms and lashed quite securely, to his own satisfaction; then he can be towed across the river with a string. If he lose courage halfway, it cannot be helped; it will do him no harm, and his swimming friend is in no danger of being grappled with and drowned. For very short distances, a usual way is for the man who cannot swim to hold his friend by the hips. A very little floating power is enough to buoy a man's head above still water.

LANDING THROUGH BREAKERS.

In landing through a heavy surf, wait for a large wave, and come in on the crest of it; then make every possible exertion to scramble up to some firm holding-place, whence its indraft, when it returns, can be resisted. If drawn back, you will be heavily battered, perhaps maimed, certainly far more exhausted than before, and not a whit nearer to safety. Avoid receiving a breaker in the attitude of scrambling away from it on hands and knees; from such a position, the wave projects a man headforemost with fearful force, and rolls him over and over in its surge. He ought to turn on his back the instant before the breaker is upon him; and then all will go well, and he will be helped on, and not half-killed by it.

☞ The chilliness consequent on staying long in water is retarded by rubbing all over the body, before entering it, about twice as much oil or bear's grease as a person uses for his hair.

Men on shore can rescue a man who is being washed to and fro in the surf, by holding together, very firmly, hand in hand, and forming a line down to the sea; the foremost man clutches the swimmer as soon as he is washed up to him, and holds him firmly while the wave is retiring. The force of the indraft is enormous and none but strong men can withstand it.

FLOATS.

If a traveler can swim pretty well, it is a good plan to make a float when he wishes to cross a river, and to lay his breast upon it, while his clothes and valuables are enclosed in a huge turban on his head. In this way, he may cross the broadest streams and float great distances down a river. He may tie paddles to his hands. His float may consist of a faggot of rushes, a log of wood, or any one of his empty water vessels, whether barrels or bags; for whatever will keep water in, will also keep it out. The small quantity of air, which might escape through the sides of a bag, should be restored by blowing afresh into it during the voyage. A few yards of intestine blown out and tied here and there, so as to form so many watertight compartments, makes a capital swimming belt; it may be wound in a figure of eight round the neck and under the armpits. When employing empty bottles, they should be well corked and made fast under the armpits, or be stuffed within the shirt or jersey, and a belt tied round the waist below them to keep them in place.

☞ The swimmer's valuables may as well be put inside the empty vessel that acts as his float, as in the turban on his head. A goatskin is often filled half full of the things he wants to carry, and is then blown out and its mouth secured. A small parcel, if tightly wrapped up in many folds, will keep dry for a long time, though partly immersed in water: the outside of it may be greased, oiled, or waxed, for additional security. If deeply immersed, the water is sure to get in.

African swimming ferry. The people of Yoruba have a singular mode of transporting passengers across rivers and streams, when the violence and rapidity of their currents prevent them from using canoes with safety. The passenger grasps the float, on the top of which his luggage is lashed; and a perfect equilibrium is preserved by the ferry-man placing himself opposite the passenger, and laying hold of both his arms. They being thus face to face, the owner of the float propels it by striking with his legs. The natives use as their

float two of their largest calabashes, cutting off their small ends and joining the openings face to face, so as to form a large, hollow, watertight vessel.

Makeshift lifebelt. A moderately effective lifebelt may be made of holland, ticking, canvas, or similar materials, in the following manner, and might be used with advantage by the crew of a vessel aground some way from the mainland, who are about to swim for their lives. Cut out two complete rings, of 16 inches outer diameter and 8 inches inner diameter; sew these together along both edges, with as fine a needle as possible and with double thread; add strong shoulder straps, so that it shall not, by any possibility, slip down over the hips; and, lastly, sew into it a long narrow tube, made out of a strip, a foot long and 2 inches wide, of the same material as the belt. At the mouth of this, a bit of wood, an inch long, with a hole bored down its middle, should be inserted as a mouthpiece. Through this tube the belt can be reinflated by the swimmer while in the water, as often as may be necessary; and, by simply twisting the tube and tucking its end in the belt, its vent can always be closed. After a canvas belt is thoroughly drenched, it will hold the air very fairly; the seams are its weakest parts.

☞ For supporting a swimmer in calm water, a collar is as good as a belt.

SWIMMING WITH HORSES.

Seize his tail, and let him tow you across

In crossing a deep river with a horse or other large animal, drive him in, or even lead him along a steep bank, and push him sideways suddenly into the water; having fairly started him, jump in yourself, seize his tail, and let him tow you across. If he turns his head with the intention of changing his course, splash water in his face with your right or left hand, as the case may be, holding the tail with one hand and splashing with the other; and you will, in this way, direct him just as you like. This is by far the best way of swimming a horse: all others are objectionable and even dangerous with animals new

to the work, such as to swim alongside the horse with one hand on his shoulder, or, worst of all, to retain your seat on his back. If this last method be persisted in, at least let the rider take his feet out of the stirrups before entering the water.

WATER SPECTACLES.

When a man opens his eyes under water, he can see nothing distinctly; but everything is as much out of focus as if he looked, in air, through a pair of powerful spectacles that were utterly unsuited to him. He cannot distinguish the letters of the largest print in a newspaper advertisement; he cannot see the spaces between the outstretched fingers, at arm's length, in clear water; nor at a few inches' distance, in water that is somewhat opaque.

I presented a short paper on this subject, at the British Association in 1865, in which I showed the precise cause of this imperfection of vision and how it might be remedied. If the front of our eyeballs had been flat, we should have had the power of seeing under water as clearly as in air; but instead of being flat, they are very convex; consequently our eye stamps a concave lens of high power into the water, and it is the seeing through this concave eyeglass which our eyeball makes for itself, that causes the indistinctness of our vision. Knowing the curvature of the eyeball, it is easy to calculate the curvature of a convex lens of flint-glass that should, when plunged into water, produce effects of an exactly equal and contrary value, exactly neutralizing the effects of the concave eyeglass of water, if it were held immediately in front of the pupil of the eye.

If the spectacle lens be of flint glass and doubly convex, each of its faces should have a curvature of not greater than 62 tenths of an inch, nor more than 82 tenths of an inch in radius; within these limits, it is practicable to obtain perfectly distinct vision under water by pressing the spectacles forwards or backwards to a moderate degree. Lenses of these high magnifying powers are sometimes sold by spectacle makers for persons who have undergone an operation for cataract. I have tried, but hitherto without much success, to arrange the fittings by which the lenses are secured so that by a move-ment of the jaw or by an elevation of the eyebrows, I could give the necessary adjustment of the glasses, leaving my hands free for the purpose of swimming.

RAFTS.

RUDE BOATS.

BOATS.

BOATING GEAR.

BOATBUILDING.

BOAT MANAGEMENT.

☞ Outriggers vastly increase
the stability of a raft.

RAFTS AND BOATS

RAFTS.

Rafts are made of logs of wood, held together
by pairs of crossbars, one of each pair lying above
the raft and the other below; then the whole may
be made quite firm by a little judicious notching
where the logs cross, and a few pegs and lashings.
Briers, woodbines, &c., will do for these. If the logs
are large, they should be separately launched into
the river, and towed into their proper places.

The raft fastening in common use *(fig. 1)* is
a stout, lithe wand, bent over the crosspiece, and
wedged into holes in the framework. The rafts
of European rivers are usually built on shore and
launched into the water; three slides are laid for
the purpose on the sloping bank of the river; upon
these are laid the four poles, secured together by
their ends, which are to form the framework of the
raft *(fig. 2)*. Other poles are put in between, until the
whole is complete.

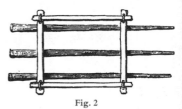

Fig. 1   Fig. 2

Floating power of various woods. The floating
power of a raft depends on the buoyancy of the
wood of which it is made. I give, in a table, a list of
the specific gravities of a few well-known woods;
and have annexed to them a column of what may

be called their "specific floating powers." Hence, to find the actual floating power of a raft, it is simply necessary to multiply its weight into the specific floating power of the wood of which it is made. Thus, a raft of twelve logs of larch, averaging 30 lbs. each, weighs 360 lbs.; this multiplied by .47 is equal to 169 lbs. very nearly, which is the weight the raft will support without sinking. Poplar is the lightest on the list.

	Specific Gravities.	Specific Floating Powers.	Factors to be multiplied into burden to find weight of raft just able to support it.
Alder	·80	·25	4·0
Ash	·85	·18	5·7
Beech	·85	·18	5·7
Elm	·59 to ·80	·70 to ·25	1·4 to 4·0
Fir	·47 to ·60	1·13 to ·66	0·9 to 1·5
Larch	·53	·89	1·1
Oak	·75	·33	3·0
„ heart of	1·17	sinks	cannot be used
Pine	·40 to ·63	1·50 to ·60	0·7 to 1·7
Poplar	·33	1·63	0·6
Willow	·59	·70	1·4

Reed rafts. Mr. Andersson, ◈ in exploring the Tioughe River in South Africa, met with two very simple forms of rafts: the one was a vast quantity of reeds cut down, heaped into a stack of from 30 to 50 feet in diameter, pushed out into the water, and allowed to float downstream; each day, as the reeds became waterlogged, more were cut and thrown on the stack; its great bulk made it sure of passing over shallow places; and when it struck against "snags," the force of the water soon slewed it round and started it afresh. On an affair of this description, Mr. Andersson, with seven attendants, and two canoes hauled up upon it, descended the river for five days.

The second reed raft was a small and neat one, and used for ferries; it was a mattress of reeds, 5 feet long, 3 broad, and some 8 inches thick, tied together

Charles John Andersson (Swedish, 1827-67), a naturalist and ornithologist, joined Galton as his second-in-command on the expedition in southwest Africa (1850-52). After Galton's departure, Andersson continued the expedition for two additional years and fulfilled its original goals; thus it is his name rather than Galton's linked to exploration of the territory now known as Namibia. After organizing a successful expedition to Lake Ngami he wrote an account of his adventures, *Lake Ngami; Or, Explorations and Discoveries, During Four Years Wanderings in the Wilds of South Western Africa* (1856), a classic travel narrative.

Sir John Henry Lefroy (British, 1817-1890), a soldier and scientist, was a pioneer in the field of terrestrial magnetism. He spent eleven years as head of the Toronto Magnetic and Meteorological Observatory and, during this time, traveled over 5,000 miles in northwestern Canada in search of the Magnetic North Pole. He later served as governor of Bermuda and Tasmania.

with strips of the reeds themselves; to each of its four corners was fixed a post made of an upright faggot of reeds 18 inches high; other faggots connected the tops of the posts horizontally, in the place of rails; this was all. It held one or two men, and nothing but reeds or rushes were used in its construction.

Rafts of distended hides.

A single ox hide may be made into a float capable of sustaining about 300 lbs.; the skin is to be cut to the largest possible circle, then gathered together round a short tube, to the inner end of which a valve, like that of a common pair of bellows, has been applied: it is inflated with bellows, and, as the air escapes by degrees, it may be refilled every ten or twelve hours. (Lefroy's ◆ Handbook for Field Service.)

We read of the skins of animals, stuffed with hay to keep them distended, having been used by Alexander the Great and by others.

Goatskin rafts are extensively used on the Tigris and elsewhere. These are inflated through one of the legs; they are generally lashed to a framework of wood, branches, and reeds in such a way that the leg is accessible to a person sitting on the raft; when the air has in part escaped, he creeps round to the skins, one after the other, untying and reinflating them in succession.

☞ In Bornu, they make large rafts, by putting a frame over several of these mákara, placed side by side.

African gourd raft. Over a large part of Bornu, especially on its Komadugu—the so-called River Yeou of Central Africa—no boat is used except the following ingenious contrivance. It is called a "mákara," or boat par éminence.

Two large open gourds are nicely balanced, and fixed, bottom downwards, on a bar or

Fig. 2　　　　　Fig. 1

yoke of light wood, 4 feet long, 4½ inches wide, and ¾ or 1 inch thick. The fisherman, or traveler, packs his gear into the gourds; launches the mákara into the river, and seats himself astride the bar. He then paddles off, with help of his hands *(fig. 1)*. When he leaves the river, he carries the mákara on his back *(fig. 2)*.

The late Dr. Barth wrote to me,

A person accustomed to such sort of voyage, sits very comfortably; a stranger holds on to one of the calabashes. There is no fear of capsizing, as the calabashes go under water, according to the weight put upon them, from ten to sixteen inches. The yoke is firmly fastened to the two calabashes, for it is never taken off. I am scarcely able, at present, to say how it is fastened. As far as I remember, it is fixed by a very firm lashing, which forms a sort of network over the calabash, and at the same time serves to strengthen the latter and guard it against an accident.

RUDE BOATS.

Brazilian sailing boat. A simpler sailing boat or raft could hardly be imagined than that shown in the figure; it is used by fishermen in Brazil. Log canoes are made by hollowing out a long tree by axe and by fire, and fastening an outrigger to one side of it to give steadiness in the water. Recollect Robinson Crusoe's◆ difficulty in launching his canoe after he had made it. It is not a difficult, though a tedious operation, to burn out hollows in wood; the fire is confined by wet earth, that it may not extend too far to either side, and the charred matter is from

Daniel Defoe's **Robinson Crusoe,** the most popular adventure tale written in the English language, was first published in 1719. The fictional protagonist was stranded "all alone in an uninhabited Island on the coast of America, near the Mouth of the Great River of Oroonoque; Having been cast on Shore by Shipwreck, wherein all the Men perished but himself." Crusoe spends five months fashioning a dugout canoe that can hold twenty-eight men; after many failed attempts at getting the canoe to water, he is forced to abandon it. Crusoe laments, "This grieved me heartily; and now I saw, though too late, the folly of beginning a work before we count the cost, and before we judge rightly of our own strength to go through with it."

Fig. 1

☞ These three-plank canoes are in frequent use in Norway. Bark may be used instead of planks.

John Charles Fremont
(1813-1890) led numerous mapping expeditions in the western U.S., including surveys of the Oregon Trail (1842), Oregon Territory (1844), and the Great Basin and Sierra Mountains (1845). He served in the Mexican-American War and the Civil War. Fremont was one of the first two U.S. senators from California, and in 1856 he was nominated as the Republican Party's first candidate for president; he ran on an anti-slavery platform and lost to James Buchanan.

time to time scraped away, and fresh fire raked back on the newly-exposed surface.

Canoe of three planks. A swift, safe, and graceful little boat, with a sharp stem and stern, and with a bottom that curves upwards at both ends, can be made out of three planks. The sketch *(fig. 1),* is a foreshortened view of the boat, and the diagram *(fig. 2)* shows the shape of the planks from which it is made. The thwart or seat shown in fig. 1 is important in giving the proper inclination to the sides of the boat, for, without it, they would tend to collapse, and the bottom would be less curved at either end.

If the reader will take the trouble to trace fig. 2 on a stout card, to cut it out in a single piece (cutting only half through the cardboard, where the planks touch), and to fasten it into shape with

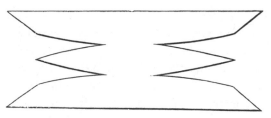

Fig. 2

pieces of gummed paper, he will understand the architecture of the boat more easily than from any description. If he wishes to build a boat he had best proceed to make as large a model in pasteboard as his materials admit, and to cut the planks to scale, according to the pattern of his model. The grace of the boat depends on the cut of its planks, just as much as the elegance of a dress does on that of its cloth.

Inflatable India-rubber boats are an invention that has proved invaluable to travelers; they have been used in all quarters of the globe and are found to stand every climate. A full-sized one weighs only 40 lbs. They have done especial service in Arctic exploration; the waters of the Great Salt Lake, in the Mormon country, were first explored and navigated with one by Fremont;◈ they were also employed by Dr. Livingstone◈ on the rivers of South Africa. They stand a wonderful amount of wear and tear, but, as boats, they are inferior to native canoes, as they are very slow in the water; it is, indeed, impossible to paddle them against a moderate headwind.

Basket boat with canvas sides. FitzRoy◈ gives an account of a party of his sailors, whose boat had been stolen while they were encamped, putting out to sea in a large basket, woven with such boughs as were at hand, and covered with their canvas tent—the inside of which they had puddled with clay to keep the water from oozing through too fast. They were eighteen hours afloat in this crazy craft. I mention this instance to show how almost anything will make a boat. Canvas saturated with grease or oil is waterproof, and painted canvas is at first an excellent covering for a boat, but it soon becomes rotten.

Canoe of reeds or vegetable fiber. A canoe may be made of reeds, rushes, or the light inner bark of trees. Either of these materials is bound into three long faggots, pointed at one end; these are placed side by side and lashed together, and the result is a serviceable vessel, of the appearance fig. 1, and section as fig. 2. Lake Titicaca, which lies far above the

David Livingstone (British, 1813-1873) arguably has remained the most famous explorer of the Victorian age—despite his failure to succeed as a missionary (he only converted one African to Christianity) and as an explorer (his expedition on the Zambezi River was recalled; and when, after seven years searching, he thought he had found the source of the Nile, he was on the Upper Congo). Yet the world was thrilled by the adventures of this Scot who had worked in a cotton mill from the age of ten; traveled to Africa as a medical missionary; became an active anti-slavery campaigner; and was the first European to see Victoria Falls and the first to cross the African continent from sea to sea. When Livingstone became ill and out of contact for six years, the world was caught up in the mystery of his whereabouts. Henry Stanley, a New York reporter, tracked him down on the shores of Lake Tanganyika and asked that marvelous question so full of polite understatement that it alone may have made Dr. Livingstone a lasting legend.

Fig. 1   Fig. 2

limit of trees, is navigated by boats made of rushes, and carrying sails woven of rushes also. Little boats are sometimes made of twigs, and are then plastered both inside and outside with clay, but they are very leaky.

Hide tray. This is a good contrivance; and if the hide be smoked after it is set, it is vastly improved. In its simplest form, Peruvian travelers describe it as a dish or tray, consisting of a dry hide pinched up at the four corners, and each corner secured with a thorn. The preferable plan is to make eyelet holes round its rim, and pass a thong through, drawing it pretty close; the tray is kept in shape by sticks put inside and athwart its bottom.

Coracle and skin punt. If a traveler has one hide only at his disposal he should make a coracle, if he has two, a punt. This last is a really useful boat; one in which very great distances of river may be de-scended with safety, and much luggage taken. Hide boats are very light, since the weight of a bullock's skin only averages 45 lbs.; but, unless well greased, they soon rot. When taken out of the water, they should be laid bottom upwards to dry.

To make a proper and substantial coracle, a dozen or more osier or other wands must be cut; these are to be bent, and have both ends stuck in the ground, in such a way as to form the framework of the required boat, bottom upwards, much like half a walnut shell in shape, but flatter. Where these wands cross, they should be lashed; and sticks should be wattled in to fill up gaps. A raw hide is then thrown over the framework, sewn in place, and left to dry. Finally, the projecting ends of the osiers have to be cut off. Should this boat, by any chance, prove a failure, the hide is not wasted, but can be removed, soaked till soft, and used again.

A skin punt requires two bullocks' or other hides, and also about ten small willow trees, or other tough flexible wood, 14 feet long. Captain Palliser says that a couple of days is sufficient for two people to complete an entire punt of this description.

> Bark boats. *"From a pine, or other tree, take off with care the longest possible entire portion of the bark; while fresh and flexible, spread it flat as a long rectangular sheet; then turn it carefully up at the sides, the smooth side outwards; sew the ends together, and caulk them well. A few cross-sticks for thwarts complete this contrivance, which is made by an American Indian in a few hours, and in which the rapid waters of the Mackenzie are navigated for hundreds of miles. Ways of strengthening the structure will readily suggest themselves. The native material for sewing is the fibrous root of the pine.* (Lieut. Col. Lefroy, Handbook for Field Service.)*

BOATS.

Of wood. English-made boats have been carried by explorers for great distances on wheels, but seldom seem to have done much useful service. They would travel easiest if slung and made fast in a strong wooden crate or framework, to be fixed on the body of the carriage. A white covering is necessary for a wooden boat on account of the sun; both boat and covering should be frequently examined. Mr. Richardson◆ and his party took a boat, divided

☞ Birch bark, as is well known, is used for building canoes in North America, and the bark of many other trees would do for covering the framework of a boat, in default of leather. But it is useless to give a detailed account of birch canoes, as great skill and neat execution are required both in making and in using them.

James Richardson (British, 1806-1851), a Protestant priest, traveled south from Tripoli on behalf of a British Bible society to investigate the slave trade among peoples of the Sahara. His resulting book, *Travels into the Great Desert of Sahara* (1849), stirred strong anti-slavery sentiment in Britain. During a second Saharan trip, from Tripoli to Lake Chad, Richardson died of an illness and his colleague Heinrich Barth took over the expedition.

MacGregor Laird (British, 1808-1861) was a Scottish merchant who established trading routes on the Niger River. He was one of nine survivors among the forty-nine who undertook the journey, and co-author of *Narrative of an Expedition into the Interior of Africa by the River Niger in 1832, 1833, 1834.*

in four quarters, on camel back across the Sahara, all the way from the Mediterranean to Lake Chad. A portable framework of metal tubes, to be covered with India rubber sheeting on arrival, was suggested to me by a very competent authority, the late Mr. M'Gregor Laird. ◈

Canoes. The earlier exploits of the 'Rob Roy' canoe justly attracted much attention, and numerous canoe voyages have subsequently been made. The Canoe Club is now a considerable institution, many of whose members make yearly improvements in the designs of their crafts. Although canoes are delicately built and apparently fragile, experience has amply proved that they can stand an extraordinary amount of hard usage in the hands of careful travelers. As a general rule, it is by no means the heaviest and most solid things that endure the best. If a lightly-made apparatus can be secured from the risk of heavy things falling upon it, it will outlast a heavy apparatus that shakes to pieces under the jar of its own weight.

As a general rule, it is by no means the heaviest and most solid things that endure the best

BOATING GEAR.

Anchors may be made of wood weighted with stones. Fig. 1 shows the anchor used by Brazilian fishermen with their rude boat or sailing raft already described. Fig. 2 shows another sort of anchor that is in common use in Norway.

Fig. 1

Mast. Where there is difficulty in "stepping" a mast, use a bar across the thwarts and two poles, one lashed at either end of it, and coming together to a point above. This triangle takes the place of the masts and is secured by shrouds fore and aft. It is a very convenient rig for a boat with an outrigger; the Sulu pirates use it.

Fig. 2

Outrigger irons. Mr. Gilby informs me that he has traveled with a pair of light sculls and outrigger irons, which he was able to adapt to many kinds of rude boats. He found them of much service in Egypt.

Keels are troublesome to make; lee-boards are effective substitutes, and are easily added to a rude boat or punt when it is desired to rig her as a sailing craft.

Rudder. A rude oar makes the most powerful, though not the most convenient, rudder. In the lakes of North Italy, where the winds are steady, the heavy boats have a bar upon which the tiller of the rudder rests; this bar is full of small notches; and the bottom of the tiller, at the place where it rests on the bar, is furnished with a blunt knife-edge; the tiller is not stiffly joined to the rudder, but admits of a little play up and down. When the boatman finds that the boat steers steadily, he simply drops the tiller, which forthwith falls into the notch below it, where it is held tight until the steersman cares to take the tiller into his hand again.

Buoys. An excellent buoy to mark out a passage is simply a small pole anchored by a rope at the end. It is very readily seen, and exposes so little surface to the wind and water, that it is not easily washed away. A pole of the thickness of a walking stick is much used in Sweden. Such a buoy costs only a rope, a stick, and a stone. A tuft of the small branches may be left on the top of the pole.

Log. For a log use a conical canvas bag thus: When the peg is drawn out by the usual jerk, the bag no longer presents its mouth to the water, but is easily drawn in by the line attached to its point.

☞ If you have an ordinary boat, and wish to make it of greater burden, saw it in half and lengthen it. Comparatively coarse carpentering is good enough for this purpose.

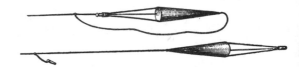

BOAT BUILDING.

Caulking. Almost anything that is fibrous does for caulking the seams of a boat. The inner bark of trees is one of the readiest materials.

Securing planks. In default of nails, it is possible to drill or to burn holes in the planks and to sew them together with strips of hide, woodbine, or string made from the inner bark of fibrous trees.

☞ By making a canvas half-deck to an open boat, you much increase its safety in broken water; and if it be made to lace down the center, it can be rolled up on the gunwale, and be out of the way in fine weather.

BOAT MANAGEMENT.

When caught by a gale recollect that a boat will lie-to and live through almost any weather, if you can make a bundle of a few spare spars, oars, &c.,

and secure them to the boat's head, so as to float in front of and across the bow. They will act very sensibly as a breakwater, and will always keep the boat's head towards the wind. Krumen rig out three oars in a triangle, lash the boat's sail to it, throw overboard, after making fast, and pay out as much line as they can muster.

In floating down a stream when the wind blows right against you (and on rivers the wind nearly always blows right up or right down), a plan generally employed is to cut large branches, to make them fast to the front of the boat, weight them that they may sink low in the water, and throw them overboard. The force of the stream acting on these branches will more than counterbalance that of the wind upon the boat. For want of branches, a kind of water sail is sometimes made of canvas.

Sail tent. A boat's sail is turned into a tent by erecting a gable-shaped framework, the mast or other spar being the ridge pole and a pair of crossed oars lashed together supporting it at either end; the whole is made stable by a couple of ropes and pegs. Then the sail is thrown across the ridge pole (not over the crossed tops of the oars, for they would fret it), and is pegged out below. The natural fall of the canvas tends to close the two ends, as with curtains.

☞ In dark nights, when on a river running through pine forests, the midstream can be kept by occasionally striking the water sharply with the blade of the oar and listening to the echoes. They should reach the ear simultaneously, or nearly so, from either bank. On the same principle, vessels have been steered out of danger when caught by a dense fog close to a rocky coast.

☞ Where these abound, travelers on rivers with overhanging branches should beware of keeping too near inshore, lest the rigging of the boat should brush down the snakes.

FORDS.

TO CROSS BOGGY AND
UNCERTAIN GROUND.

BRIDGES.

☞ Rivers cannot be forded
if their depth exceeds 3 feet for
men or 4 feet for horses.

FORDS AND BRIDGES

FORDS.

Fords are easily discovered by tying a sounding pole to the stern of a boat rowing down the middle of the stream and searching those places where the pole touches the bottom. When no boat is to be had, fords should be tried for where the river is broad rather than where it is narrow, and especially at those places where there are bends in its course. In these the line of shallow water does not run straight across, but follows the direction of a line connecting a promontory on one side to the nearest promontory on the other, as in the drawing; that is to say, from A to B, or from B to C, and not right across from B to *b*, from A to *a*, or from C to *c*.

Along hollow curves, as at *a, b, c,* the stream runs deep, and usually beneath overhanging banks; whilst in front of promontories, as at A, B, and C, the water is invariably shoal, unless it be a jutting rock that makes the promontory. Therefore, by entering the stream at one promontory, with the intention of leaving it at another, you ensure that at all events the beginning and end of your course shall be in shallow water, which you cannot do by attempting any other line of passage.

TO CROSS BOGGY AND UNCERTAIN GROUND.

Swamps. When you wish to take a wagon across a deep, miry, and reedy swamp, outspan and let the cattle feed. Then cut faggots of reeds and strew them thickly over the line of intended passage. When plenty are laid down, drive the cattle backwards and forwards, and they will trample them in. Repeat the process two or three times, till the causeway is firm enough to bear the weight of the wagon. Or, in default of reeds, cut long poles and several short crossbars, say of 2 feet long; join these as best you can, so as to make a couple of ladder-shaped frames. Place these across the mud, one under the intended track of each wheel. Faggots strewn between each round of the ladder will make the causeway more sound. A succession of logs, laid crosswise with faggots between them, will also do, but not so well.

☞ In fording a swift stream, carry heavy stones in your hands, for you require weight to resist the force of the current: indeed, the deeper you wade, the more weight you require, though you have so much the less at command, on account of the water buoying you up.

Passing from hand to hand. When many things have to be conveyed across a piece of abominably bad road—as over sand dunes, heavy shingle, mud of 2 feet deep, a morass, a jagged mountain tract, or over stepping stones in the bed of a rushing torrent—it is a great waste of labor to make laden men travel to and fro with loads on their backs. It is a severe exertion to walk at all under these circumstances, letting alone the labor of also carrying a burden. The men should be stationed in a line, each at a distance of 6 or 7 feet from his neighbor, and should pass the things from hand to hand, as they stand.

Snow. Sir R. Dalyell tells me that it is the practice of muleteers in the neighborhood of Erzurum, when their animals lose their way and flounder in the deep snow, to spread a horse-cloth or other thick rug from off their packs upon the snow in front of them. The animals step upon it and

☞ Water that is slightly
frozen is made to bear a heavy
wagon by cutting reeds, strew-
ing them thickly on the ice,
and pouring water upon them;
when the whole is frozen into a
firm mass the process must be
repeated.

Sir Howard Douglas (British,
1776-1861), an army general,
spent his entire career in the
military, beginning with the
Royal Artillery at age eighteen.
He was a founder of the Royal
Geographic Society.

extricate themselves easily. I have practiced walking
across deep snowdrifts on this principle, with perfect
success.

BRIDGES.

Fledges are well known: a long cord or chain
of poles is made fast to a rock or an anchor in the
middle of a river. The other end is attached to the
ferryboat, which being so slewed as to receive the
force of the current obliquely, traverses the river
from side to side.

Bridges of felled trees. If you are at the side of a
narrow but deep and rapid river, on the banks of
which trees grow long enough to reach across, one
or more may be felled, confining the trunk to its
own bank and letting the current force the head
round to the opposite side; but if

*the river be too wide to be spanned by one tree—and if two
or three men can in any manner be got across—let a large
tree be felled into the water on each side, and placed close
to the banks opposite to each other, with their heads lying
up-streamwards. Fasten a rope to the head of each tree,
confine the trunks, shove the head off to receive the force
of the current, and ease off the ropes, so that the branches
may meet in the middle of the river at an angle pointing
upwards. The branches of the trees will be jammed together
by the force of the current, and so be sufficiently united as
to form a tolerable communication, especially when a few of
the upper branches have been cleared away. If insufficient,
towards the middle of the river, to bear the weight of men
crossing, a few stakes with forks left near their heads, may
be thrust down through the branches of the trees to support
them. (Sir H. Douglas. ◈)*

WATER FOR DRINKING

In most of those countries where traveling is arduous, it is the daily care of an explorer to obtain water for his own use and for that of his caravan. Should he be traveling in regions that are for the most part arid and rarely visited by showers, he must look for his supplies in ponds made by the drainage of a large extent of country, or in those left here and there along the beds of partly dried-up watercourses, or in fountains. If he be unsuccessful in his search, or when the dry season of the year has advanced and all water has disappeared from the surface of the land, there remains no alternative for him but to dig wells where there are marks to show that pools formerly lay, or where there are other signs that well water may be obtained.

Purity of watering places. Make no litter by the side of watering places, and encourage among your party the Mohammedan feeling of respect for preserving the purity of drinking water. Old travelers commonly encamp at a distance from the watering place and fetch the water to their camp.

SIGNS OF THE NEIGHBORHOOD OF WATER.

The quick intelligence with which experienced travelers discover watering places is so great that it might almost be mistaken for an instinct.

Intelligence of dogs and cattle. Dogs are particularly clever in finding water, and the fact of a dog looking refreshed, and it may be wet, has often drawn attention to a pond that would otherwise

SIGNS OF THE NEIGHBORHOOD OF WATER.

POOLS OF WATER.

FOUNTAINS.

WELLS.

DISTILLED WATER.

OCCASIONAL MEANS OF QUENCHING THIRST.

TO PURIFY WATER THAT IS MUDDY OR PUTRID.

THIRST, TO RELIEVE.

CARRYING WATER.

☞ I may here remark that it is a good general rule for an explorer of an arid country, when he happens to come to water, after not less than three hours' traveling, to stop and encamp by it; it is better for him to avail himself of his good fortune and be content with his day's work, than to risk the uncertainty of another supply.

have been overlooked and passed by. Cattle are very uncertain in their intelligence. Sometimes oxen go for miles and miles across a country unknown to them, straight to a pond of water; at other times they are most obtuse. Dr. Leichhardt,◆ the Australian traveler, was quite astonished at their stupidity in this respect.

Trees and ordinary vegetation are not of much help in directing a traveler to water, for they thrive on dew or on occasional rain, but it is otherwise when the vegetation is unusually green or luxuriant, or when those trees are remarked that are seldom seen to grow except near water in the particular country visited, as the blackthorn tree in South Africa.

Birds. Some species of birds (as water fowl, parrots, and the diamond bird) or animals (as baboons) afford surer promise; but the converging flight of birds, or the converging fresh tracks of animals, is the most satisfactory sign of all. It is about nightfall that desert birds usually drink, and hence it often happens that the exhausted traveler, abandoning all hope as the shades of evening close in, has his attention arrested by flights of birds that give him new life and tell him where to go.

Tracks. In tropical countries that have rainy and dry seasons, it must be recollected that old paths of men or wild animals only mislead; they go to dry ponds that were full at the time they were trodden, but have since been abandoned on becoming exhausted.

POOLS OF WATER.

For many days after there has been rain, water is sure to be found among mountains, however desert may be their appearance; for not only does more wet fall upon them, but the drainage is more perfect. Long after the ravines and streambeds are quite dry, puddles and cupfuls of water will be found here and there along their courses, in holes and chinks and under great stones, which together form a sufficiency. A sponge tied to the end of a stick will do good service in lapping these up.

The sandy beds of watercourses in arid countries frequently contain pools of stagnant water; but the places where these pools are to be found are not necessarily those where they have been found in preceding years. The conditions necessary for the existence of a pool are not alone those of the rocky substratum of the riverbed, but, more especially, the stratifications of mud and clay left after each flooding. For instance, an extensive bed of sand, enclosed between two layers of clay, would remain moist and supply well water during the dry season; but a trivial variation in the force and amount of the current, in different years, might materially affect the place and the character of the deposition of these clay strata.

In searching the beds of partly dried-up watercourses, the fact must never be forgotten that it is especially in little tributaries at the point where they fall into the main one that most water is to be found, and the most insignificant of these should never be overlooked. I presume that the bar, which always accumulates in front of tributaries, and is formed of numerous layers of alluvial deposit,

☞ Well water may be sought where the earth is still moist, though arid all around, or, failing that, where birds and wild animals have lately been scratching, or where gnats hover in swarms.

☞ From the number of birds, tracks, and other signs, travelers are often pretty sure that they are near water, but cannot find the spring itself. In this case the party should at once be spread out as skirmishers, and the dogs cheered on.

☞ It is usual, when no damp earth can be seen, but where the place appears likely to yield well water, to force an iron ramrod deep into the soil, and, if it bring up any grains that are moist, to dig.

☞ When a riverbed has been long followed by a traveler, and a frequent supply of water found along it, in pools or even in wells, say at every 5 or 10 miles—then, should this riverbed appear to lose itself in a plain that is arid, there is no reason why the traveler should be disheartened; for, on traveling further, the water will be sure to be found again, those plains being always green and grassy where the water in such riverbeds entirely disappears.

parallel to the bed of the great stream, is very likely to have one, at least, of its layers of an impervious character. If so, the bar would shut in the wet sand of the tributary like a wall, and prevent it from draining itself dry.

By seashore. Fresh water is frequently to be found under the very sands of the seashore, whither it has oozed underground from the upper country, and where it overlies the denser salt water; or else abuts against it, if the compactness of the sand resists free percolation. In very many places along the skirt of the great African desert, fresh water is to be found by digging 2 or 3 feet.

FOUNTAINS.

Fountains in arid lands are as godsends. They are far more numerous and abundant in limestone districts than in any others, owing to the frequent fissures of those rocks; therefore, whenever limestone crops out in the midst of sand deserts, a careful search should be made for water. In granite, and other primary rocks, many but small springs are usually seen.

WELLS.

Digging wells. In default of spades, water is to be dug for with a sharp-pointed stick. Take it in both hands and, holding it upright like a dagger, stab and dig it in the ground *(fig. 1)*; then clear out the loose earth with the hand *(fig. 2)*. Continue thus working with the stick and hand alternately, and a hole as deep as the arm is easily made. In digging a large hole or well, the earth must be loosened in precisely the same manner, handed up to the surface and carried off by means of a bucket or bag, in default of a shovel and wheelbarrow.

After digging deeply, the sand will often be found just moist, no water actually lying in the well; but do not, therefore, be disheartened; wait a while, and the water will collect. After it has once begun to ooze through the sides of the well, it will continue to do so much more freely. Therefore, on arriving at night with thirsty cattle at a well of doubtful character, deepen it at once, by torchlight, that the water may have time to collect; then the cattle may be watered in the early morning and sent to feed before the sun is hot.

Fig. 1

Fig. 2

Kerkari. I am indebted to correspondents for an account of a method employed in the plains of the Sikkim Himalaya, and in Assam, where it is called a "kerkari," also in lower Bengal, for digging deep holes. The natives take a freshly cut bamboo, say 3 inches in diameter; they cut it just above one of the knots, and then split the wood as far as to the next joint in about a dozen places, and point the pieces somewhat. The other end of the instrument should be cut slantingly, to thrust into the earth to loosen it; in order to give it strength, the cut should be made obliquely through a joint and not beyond it, as in the figure. The grass is then torn away from the ground, the cut end of the bamboo is well stabbed into the earth, and its other end is afterwards worked vertically with both hands. The soft soil is thus forced into the hollow of the bamboo and spreads out its blades, as is intended to be shown in the figure. The bamboo is next withdrawn and the

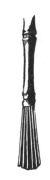

plug of earth is shaken out; it is then reintroduced and worked up and down as before. It is usual to drive a stake in the ground to act as a toothed comb, to comb out the plug of earth.

Snow water. It is impossible for men to sustain life by eating snow or ice, instead of drinking water. They only aggravate the raging torments of thirst, instead of assuaging them, and hasten death. That eating large quantities of snow should seriously disturb the animal system is credible enough, when we consider the very large amount of heat that must be abstracted from the stomach in order to melt it. Among dogs, the Eskimo is the only breed that can subsist on snow as an equivalent for water. The Arctic animals, generally, have the same power. But, as regards mankind, some means of melting snow into water, for the purposes of drinking, is an essential condition of life in the Arctic regions.

☞ It takes in practice about as long to melt snow of a low temperature into water, as it does to cause that same water to boil.

DISTILLED WATER.

It will take six or seven times as long to convert a kettle full of boiling water into steam, as it did to make that kettle boil. Hence, it is of no use to attempt to distill until you have provided abundance of good firewood of a fit size to burn quickly, and have built an efficient fireplace on which to set the kettle. Unfortunately, fuel is commonly deficient in those places where there is a lack of fresh water.

The simplest way to distill, but a very imperfect one, is to light a fire among stones near a hollow in a rock that is filled, or can be filled, with salt water. When the stones are red-hot, drop them one by one into it: the water will hiss and give out clouds of

☞ Rate of distillation: A drop per second is fully equivalent to an imperial pint of water in three hours, or to an imperial gallon in an entire day and night.

vapor, some of which may be collected in a cloth, and wrung or sucked out of it. In the same way a pot on the fire may have a cloth stretched over it to catch the steam.

Still, made with earthen pots and a metal basin. A very simple distilling apparatus is used in Bhutan; the sketch will show the principle on which it is constructed. Salt water is placed in a pot set over the fire. Another vessel, but without top or bottom, (which, for the convenience of illustration, I have indicated in the sketch by nothing more than a dotted line), is made to stand upon the pot. It serves as a support for a metal basin, which is filled with salt water, and acts as a condenser. When the pot boils, the steam ascends and condenses itself on the under surface of the basin, whence it drops down and is collected in a cup that is supported by a rude tripod of sticks, standing in the inside of the iron pot.

OCCASIONAL MEANS OF QUENCHING THIRST.

A shower of rain will yield a good supply. The clothes may be stripped off and spread out and the rainwater sucked from them. Or, when a storm is approaching, a cloth or blanket may be made fast by its four corners, and a quantity of bullets thrown in the middle of it; they will cause the water that it receives to drain to one point and trickle through the cloth into a cup or bucket set below.

☞ It must be remembered that thirst is greatly relieved by the skin being wetted, and therefore it is well for a man suffering from thirst to strip to the rain.

Seawater. Lives of sailors have more than once been saved when turned adrift in a boat, by bathing frequently and keeping their clothes damp with salt water. However, after some days, the nauseous taste of the salt water is very perceptible in the saliva, and

☞ A reversed umbrella will catch water; but the first drippings from it, or from clothes that have been long unwashed, as from a macintosh cloak, are intolerably nauseous and very unwholesome.

☞ Rainwater is lodged for some days in the huge pitcher-like corollas of many tropical flowers.

at last becomes unbearable; such, at least, was the experience of the surgeon of the wrecked *Pandora*.

Dew water is abundant near the seashore, and may be collected in the same way as rainwater. The storehouse at Angra Pequena, in S. W. Africa, in 1850, was entirely supplied by the dew water deposited on its roof. The Australians who live near the sea go among the wet bushes with a great piece of bark and brush into it the dewdrops from the leaves with a wisp of grass, collecting in this way large quantities of water. Eyre used a sponge for the same purpose, and appears to have saved his life by its use.

Animal fluids are resorted to in emergencies, such as the contents of the paunch of an animal that has been shot; its taste is like sweetwort. Mr. Darwin writes of people who, catching turtles, drank the water that was found in their pericardia; it was pure and sweet. Blood will stand in the stead of solid food, but it is of no avail in the stead of water, on account of its saline qualities.

Vegetable fluids. Many roots exist from which both natives and animals obtain a sufficiency of sap and pulp, to take the place of water. The traveler should inquire of the natives, and otherwise acquaint himself with those peculiar to the country that he visits, such as the roots which the eland eats, the bitter watermelon, &c.

TO PURIFY WATER THAT IS MUDDY OR PUTRID.

With muddy water, the remedy is to filter, and to use alum if you have it. With putrid, to boil, to mix with charcoal, or expose to the sun and air; or what is best, to use all three methods at the same time. When the water is salt or brackish, nothing avails but distillation.

To filter muddy water. When, at the watering place, there is little else but a mess of mud and filth, take a good handful of grass or rushes and tie it roughly together in the form of a cone, 6 or 8 inches long; then dipping the broad end into the puddle, and turning it up, a streamlet of fluid will trickle down through the small end. This excellent plan is used by the Northern Bushmen—at their wells quantities of these bundles are found lying about. (Andersson.) Otherwise suck water through your handkerchief by putting it over the mouth of your mug, or by throwing it on the gritty mess as it lies in the puddle.

THIRST, TO RELIEVE.

Thirst is a fever of the palate which may be somewhat relieved by other means than drinking fluids.

By exciting saliva. The mouth is kept moist, and thirst is mitigated, by exciting the saliva to flow. This can be done by chewing something, as a leaf, or by keeping in the mouth a bullet, or a smooth, non-absorbent stone such as a quartz pebble.

By fat or butter. In Australia, Africa, and N. America, it is a frequent custom to carry a small quantity of fat or butter, and to eat a spoonful at a time, when the thirst is severe. These act on the irritated membranes of the mouth and throat, just as cold cream upon chapped hands.

☞ Sand, charcoal, sponge, and wool are the substances most commonly used in properly constructed filters: peat charcoal is excellent. Charcoal acts not only as a mechanical filter for solid impurities, but it has the further advantage of absorbing putrid gases.

☞ Snow is used as a filter in the Arctic regions. Dr. Rae used to lay it on the water, until it was considerably higher than its level, and then to suck the water through the snow.

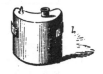

☞ On giving water to persons nearly dead from thirst: give a little at a time, let them take it in spoonfuls; for the large drafts that their disordered instincts suggest, disarrange the weakened stomach: they do serious harm, and no corresponding good. Keep the whole body wet.

By salt water. People may live long without drinking if they have means of keeping their skin constantly wet with water, even though it be salt or otherwise undrinkable. A traveler may tie a handkerchief wetted with salt water round his neck.

By checking evaporation. The Arabs keep their mouths covered with a cloth in order to prevent the sense of thirst caused by the lips being parched.

By diet. Drink well before starting and make a habit of drinking only at long intervals, and then, plenty at a time.

CARRYING WATER.

People drink excessively in hot dry climates, as the evaporation from the skin is enormous and must be counterbalanced. Under these circumstances the daily ration of a European is at least two quarts. To make an exploring expedition in such countries efficient, there should be means of carrying at least one gallon of water for each man. In unknown lands this quantity should be carried on from every watering place, so long as means can possibly be obtained for carrying it, and should be served out thus: two quarts the first day, in addition to whatever private store the men may have chosen to carry for themselves; a quart and a half during the second day; and half a quart on the morning of the third, which will carry them through that day without distress.

Besides water vessels sufficient for carrying what I have mentioned, there ought to be others for the purpose of leaving water buried in the ground, as a store for the return of a reconnoitering expedition; also each man should be furnished with a small

☞ Sir S. Baker says of the people of Unyoro, "During a journey, a pretty, bottle-shaped, long-necked gourd is carried with a store of plantain-cider; the mouth of the bottle is stopped with a bundle of the white rush shreds, through which a reed is inserted that reaches to the bottom: thus the drink can be sucked up during the march, without the necessity of halting; nor is it possible to spill it by the movement of walking."

water vessel of some kind or other for his own use, and should be made to take care of it.

Calabashes and other gourds, coconuts and ostrich eggs are all of them excellent for flasks. The Bushmen of South Africa make great use of ostrich shells as water vessels. They have stations at many

places in the desert where they bury these shells filled with water, corked with grass, and occasionally waxed over. They thus go without hesitation over wide tracts, for their sense of locality is so strong that they never fear to forget the spot in which they have dug their hiding place.

Open buckets, for carrying water for short distances, or for storing it in camp, may be made of the bark of a tree, either taken off in an entire cylinder and having a bottom fitted on, or else of a knot or excrescence that has been cut off the outside of a tree and its woody interior scooped out; or of birch bark sewed or pegged at the corners, and having its seams coated with the gum or resin of the pine tree. Baskets with oiled cloth inside make efficient water vessels; they are in use in France as firemen's buckets.

Drinking, when riding or walking. It is an awkward matter to drink when jolting on wheels, on horseback, or on foot. I adopted the plan of carrying a piece of small India-rubber tubing 6 or 8 inches long, and when I wished to drink, I removed the stopper and inserted the tube, just as an insect might let down its proboscis, and sucked the contents.

☞ When a Dutchman or a Namaqua wants to carry a load of ostrich eggs to or from the watering place, or when he robs a nest, he takes off his trousers, ties up the ankles, puts the eggs in the legs, and carries off his load slung round his neck.

☞ Watertight pots are made on the Snake River by winding long tough roots in a spiral manner and lashing the coils to one another, just as is done in making a beehive.

☞ When carrying water in buckets, put a wreath of grass, or something else that will float, on the water to prevent it from splashing; and also make a hoop inside which the porter may walk while his laden hands rest on its rim: the hoop keeps his hands wide from his body, and prevents the buckets from knocking against his legs.

THE NUTRTIVE ELEMENTS
 OF FOOD.

FOOD SUITABLE FOR THE
STORES OF TRAVELERS.

CONDIMENTS.

WHOLESOME FOOD,
PROCURABLE IN THE BUSH.

REVOLTING FOOD, THAT MAY
SAVE THE LIVES OF STARVING
MEN.

TOUGH MEAT.

THEORY OF TEA-MAKING.

FIREPLACES FOR COOKING.

OVENS.

Robert O'Hara Burke (British, 1821-1861) and **William John Wills** (British, 1834-1861) died of starvation while competing for a prize offered to the first persons who could cross Australia from south to north.
    Allen Gardiner (British, 1794-1851), a naval captain-turned-missionary, and his party lived for months without provisions at the southern end of Patagonia, eating mice, a dead fox, a penguin, and seaweed before succumbing.

FOOD

THE NUTRITIVE ELEMENTS OF FOOD.

Many chemists have applied themselves in recent years to discover the exact percentage of nutriment contained in different substances, and to determine the minimum nutriment on which human life can be supported. The results are not very accordant, but nevertheless a considerable approximation to truth has been arrived at. It is now possible to tell whether a proposed diet has any great faults of excess or deficiency, and how to remedy those faults. But it also must be recollected that the stomach is an assimilating machine of limited performance and must be fed with food that it can digest; it is not enough that the food should contain nutritious matter if that matter should be in an indigestible form. Burke◆ and Wills◆ perished from sheer inability to digest the seeds upon which the Australian savages lived; and Gardiner's◆ party died of starvation in Tierra del Fuego because they could not digest the shellfish which form a common article of diet of the natives of that country.

FOOD SUITABLE FOR THE STORES OF TRAVELERS.

The most portable kind of food is, unquestionably, the flesh of cattle, for the beasts carry themselves. The draft oxen used in African and Australian explorations serve as a last resource when all other food is wanting.

The kinds of food that are the most portable in the ordinary sense of the term are: pemmican, meat biscuit, dried meat, dried fish, wheat flour, biscuit, oatmeal, barley, peas, cheese, sugar, preserved potatoes, and Chollet's compressed vegetables.

Pemmican; general remarks. Of all food usually carried on expeditions, none is so complete in itself, nor contains so large a proportion of nutriment, as pemmican. It is especially useful to those who undergo severe work in cold and rainy climates. It is the mainstay of Arctic expeditions, whether on water, by sledge, or on foot. But, though excellent to men who are working laboriously, it is distasteful to others.

Pemmican is a mixture of about five-ninths of pounded dry meat to four-ninths of melted or boiled grease; it is put into a skin bag or tin can whilst warm and soft. The grease ought not to be very warm when poured on the dry meat. Wild berries are sometimes added. The pemmican is chopped out with an axe, when required.

Pemmican, as made in the prairie. Mr. Ballantyne, ◆ who was in the service of the Hudson's Bay Company, gives the following account:

Having shot a buffalo, the hunters cut lumps of his flesh, and slitting it up into flakes or layers, hang it up in the sun, or before a slow fire, to dry; and the fat can be dried as well as the lean. When dry, the meat is pounded between two stones till it is broken into small pieces: these are put into a bag made of the animal's hide, with the hair on the outside, and well mixed with melted grease; the top of the bag is then sewn up, and the pemmican allowed to cool. In this state it may be eaten uncooked; but the men who subsist on it when traveling, mix it with a little flour and water, and then boil it—in which state it is known throughout the country by the elegant name of robbiboo. Pemmican is good wholesome food; will keep fresh for a great length of time; and, were it not for its unprepossessing appearance, and a good many buffalo hairs mixed with it,

☞ It has been truly remarked with reference to Australian exploring expeditions that if an exploring party would make up their minds to eat horseflesh, stores of provisions might be largely dispensed with. A few extra horses could be taken and one shot occasionally, and its flesh dried and slightly salted, sufficiently to preserve it from becoming tainted before the men could consume it.

From the ages of sixteen to twenty-two, **Robert Michael Ballantyne** (British, 1825-1894) served as a Hudson's Bay Company clerk at the Red River Settlement. A loosely autobiographical adventure story based on his time in Canada, titled *The Young Fur Traders* (1856), launched Ballantyne on a successful career as author of a series of eighty novels for young people, gripping tales of escapades and survival in remote locales such as African jungles and the wild American West.

through the carelessness of the hunters, would be very palatable. After a time, however, one becomes accustomed to these little peculiarities.

Meat biscuit. Meat biscuit, which is used in American ships, is stated to be a thick soup evaporated down to a syrup, kneaded with flour, and made into biscuits: these are pricked with holes, dried and baked. They can be eaten just as they are, or made into a porridge, with from twenty to thirty times their weight of water.

Dried meat. When more game is shot than can be eaten before the party travel onwards, it is usual to jerk a part of it. It is cut in long strips and festooned about the bushes, under the full sun, in order to dry it. After it has been sun dried it will keep for long, before it becomes wholly putrid. Dried meat is a poor substitute for fresh meat; it requires long steeping in water to make it tender, and then it is tasteless and comparatively innutritious.

Dried fish. Fish may be pounded entire, just as they come from the river, dried in the sun in large lumps, and kept: the negroes about the Niger do this.

Flour travels conveniently in strong canvas bags, each holding 50 lbs., and long enough to be lashed onto a pack saddle.

CONDIMENTS.

The most portable and useful condiments for a traveler are salt, red pepper, Harvey's sauce, lime juice, dried onions, and curry powder. They should be bought at a first-rate shop; red pepper, lime juice, and curry powder are often atrociously adulterated.

☞ One man in every party should have learnt from a professed butcher how to cut up a carcass to the best advantage.

☞ The American buccaneers acquired their name from *boucan*, which means jerked meat in an Indian dialect; for they provisioned their ships with the dried flesh of the wild cattle that they hunted down and killed.

Salt. The craving for salt (chloride of sodium) is somewhat satisfied by the potash salts and, perhaps, by other minerals: thus we often hear of people reduced to the mixing of gunpowder with their food on account of the saltpeter that it contains. An impure salt is made widely in North Africa from wood ashes. They are put into a pot, hot water is poured over them and allowed to stand and dissolve out the salts they contain; the ley is then decanted into another pot, where it is evaporated. The plants in use are those of which the wetted ashes have a saline and not an alkaline taste, nor a soapy feel.

☞ In countries where salt is never used, as I myself have witnessed in South Africa, and among the Mandan North-American Indian tribes (Catlin), the soil and springs are "brack."

☞ People who eat nothing but meat feel the craving for salt far less strongly than those who live wholly on vegetables.

WHOLESOME FOOD, PROCURABLE IN THE BUSH.

Eggs may be dried at a gentle heat, then pounded and preserved. This is a convenient plan of making a store of portable food out of the eggs of seabirds, or those of ostriches.

Fish roe is another kind of portable food. The chemists declare its composition to be nearly identical with that of ordinary eggs. (Pereira.) Long narrow bags of strong linen, and a strong brine, are prepared. The bags are half-filled with the roe and are then quite filled with the brine, which is allowed to ooze through slowly. This being done, the men wring the bags strongly with their hands, and the roe is allowed to dry. Roe broth is a good dish.

☞ Four Russian sailors who were wrecked on Spitzbergen, and whose well-known adventures are to be found in *Pinkerton's Voyages and Travels,* had nothing whatever for six years to subsist on—save only the animals they killed, a little moss, and melted snowwater. One of them died; the others enjoyed robust health.

Honey, to find, when bees are seen. Dredge as many bees as you can with flour from a pepperbox; or else catch one of them, tie a feather or a straw to his leg, which can easily be done (natives thrust it up into his body), throw him into the air, and follow him as he flies slowly to his hive; or

*Carrion is
not noxious to
starving men*

☞ If any meat that you may
find, or if the water of any pool
at which you encamp, is under
suspicion of being poisoned,
let one of your dogs eat or
drink before you do, and wait
an hour to watch the effects of
it upon him.

catch two bees, and turning them loose at some distance apart, search the place towards which their flights converge. But if bees are too scarce for either of these methods, choose an open place and lay in it a plate of syrup as a bait for the bees; after one has fed and flown away again, remove the plate 200 yards in the direction in which he flew, and proceed in the same sort of way until the nest is found.

Honey bird. The instinct of the honey bird is well known, which induces him to lead men to hives that he may share in the plunder. The stories that are told of the apparent malice of the bird, in sometimes tricking a man and leading him to the lair of wild animals, instead of to the bees' nest, are well authenticated.

REVOLTING FOOD, THAT MAY SAVE THE LIVES OF STARVING MEN.

Carrion is not noxious to starving men. In reading the accounts of travelers who have suffered severely from want of food, a striking fact is common to all, namely that under those circumstances, carrion and garbage of every kind can be eaten without the stomach rejecting it. Life can certainly be maintained on a revolting diet that would cause a dangerous illness to a man who was not compelled to adopt it by the pangs of hunger. There is, moreover, a great difference in the power that different people possess of eating rank food without being made ill by it. It appears that no flesh, and very few fish, are poisonous to man; but vegetables are frequently poisonous.

Dead animals, to find. The converging flight of

crows, and gorged vultures sitting on trees, show where dead game is lying, but it is often very difficult to find the carcass, for animals usually crawl under some bush or other hiding place to die. Jackal tracks, &c., are often the only guide. It may be advisable, after an unsuccessful search, to remove to some distance and watch patiently throughout the day until the birds return to their food, and mark them down.

Rank birds. When rank birds are shot, they should be skinned, not plucked, for much of the rankness lies in their skin; or, if unskinned, they should be buried for some hours, because earth absorbs the oil that makes them rank. Their breast and wings are the least objectionable parts, and if there be abundance of food, should alone be cooked.

☞ Rank seabirds, when caught, put in a coop, and fed with corn, were found by Captain Bligh to become fat and well-tasted.

Skins. All old hides or skins of any kind that are not tanned are fit and good for food; they improve soup by being mixed with it, or they may be toasted and hammered. Long boiling would make glue or gelatin of them. Many a hungry person has cooked and eaten his sandals or skin clothing.

Bones contain a great deal of nourishment which is got at by boiling them, pounding their ends between two stones, and sucking them. There is a revolting account in French history of a besieged garrison of Sancerre, in the time of Charles IX, and again subsequently at Paris, and it may be elsewhere, digging up the graveyards for bones as sustenance.

Blood from live animals. The Aliab tribe, who have great herds of cattle on the White Nile,

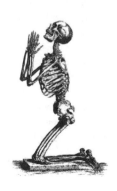

James Bruce (British, 1730-1794) was author of the five-volume *Travels to Discover the Source of the Nile in the Years 1768-73,* considered scarcely credible when issued, but subsequently deemed an accurate and informative contribution to geographic literature.

☞ When I traveled in South-West Africa, at one part of my journey a plague of bush ticks attacked the roots of my oxen's tails. Their bites made festering sores, which ended in some of the tails dropping bodily off. I heard such accidents were not at all uncommon. The animals did not travel the worse for it. Now oxtail soup is proverbially nutritious.

not only milk their cows, but they bleed their cattle periodically, and boil the blood for food. Driving a lance into a vein in the neck, they bleed the animal copiously, which operation is repeated about once a month. (Sir S. Baker.)

Flesh from live animals. The truth of Bruce's◈ well-known tale of the Abyssinians and others occasionally slicing out a piece of a live ox for food is sufficiently confirmed. Thus Dr. Beke◈ observes,

There could be no doubt of the fact. He had questioned hundreds of natives on the subject, and though at first they positively declared the statement to be a lie, many, on being more closely questioned, admitted the possibility of its truth, for they could not deny that cattle are frequently attacked by hyenas, whose practice is to leap on the animals from behind and at once begin devouring the hind quarters; and yet, if driven off in time, the cattle have still lived.

It is reasonable enough that a small worn-out party should adopt this plan, when they are traveling in a desert where the absence of water makes it impossible to delay, and when they are sinking for want of food. If the ox were killed outright there would be material for one meal only, because a worn-out party would be incapable of carrying a load of flesh. By the Abyssinian plan the wounded beast continues to travel with the party, carrying his carcass that is destined to be turned into butcher's meat for their use at a further stage. Of course the idea is very revolting, for the animal must suffer as much as the average of the tens or hundreds of wounded hares and pheasants that are always left among the bushes after an ordinary English battue. To be sure, the Abyssinian plan should only be adopted to save human life.

Insects. Most kinds of creeping things are eatable, and are used by the Chinese. Locusts and grasshoppers are not at all bad. To prepare them, pull off the legs and wings and roast them with a little grease in an iron dish, like coffee. Even the gnats that swarm on the Shire River are collected by the natives and pressed into cakes.

Wholesome and poisonous plants. No certain rule can be given to distinguish wholesome plants from poisonous ones, but it has been observed that much the same thing suits the digestion of a bird that suits that of a man; and, therefore, that a traveler, who otherwise would make trials at haphazard, ought to examine the contents of those birds' crops that he may catch or shoot, to give a clue to his experiments. The rule has notable exceptions, but in the absence of any other guide it is a very useful one.

The only general rules that botany can give are vague and full of exceptions: they are, that a great many wholesome plants are found among the Cruciferae, or those whose petals are arranged like a Maltese cross, and that many poisonous ones are found amongst the Umbelliferae. There are two moderately nutritious plants—nettle and fern—that are found wild in very many countries.

TOUGH MEAT.

Hammer it well between two stones before putting it on the fire, and again when it is half cooked, to separate the fibers. I have often seen people save themselves much painful mastication by hammering at each separate piece of meat before putting it in their mouths.

Dr. Charles Tilstone Beke (British, 1800-1874) was a businessman and geographer who wrote several books about his explorations of the Nile's sources and tributaries. He mapped 70,000 square miles of Ethiopia and the course of the Blue Nile, explored by Bruce seventy years earlier.

☞ Several kinds of seaweed, such as laver and Irish moss, are eatable.

☞ "Four expert men slice up a full-grown buffalo in four hours and a half." (Leichhardt.)

All people can ensure uniformity of good tea by attending to the principle of making it—that is to say, to time, and quantities, and temperature. There is no other mystery in the teapot

Kabobs. Broil the rib bones, or skewer your iron ramrod through a dozen small lumps of meat and roast them. This is the promptest way of cooking meat, but men on hard work are not satisfied with a diet of nothing else but tough roasted flesh; they crave for succulent food, such as boiled or baked meat.

THEORY OF TEA MAKING.

I have made a number of experiments on the art of making good tea. We constantly hear that some people are good and others bad tea makers; that it takes a long time to understand the behavior of a new teapot, and so forth; and, lastly, that good tea cannot be made except with boiling water. Now, this latter assertion is assuredly untrue, because, if tea be actually boiled in water, an emetic and partly poisonous drink is the certain result.

After numerous days in which I made tea according to my usual method, but measuring strictly the quantity of leaves, and recording the times and the temperature, and noting the character of tea produced; then, taking as my type of excellence, tea that was full bodied, full tasted, and in no way bitter or flat, I found that this was only produced when the water in the teapot had remained between 180° and 190° Fahr., and had stood eight minutes on the leaves. It was only necessary for me to add water once to the tea to ensure this temperature. Bitterness was the certain result of greater heat or of longer standing, and flatness was the result of colder water. If the tea did not stand for so long a time as eight minutes, it was not ripe; it was not full bodied enough. The palate becomes far less fastidious about the quality of the second cup. Other people may like tea of a different character from that which I do myself; but, be that as it may, all people can, I maintain, ensure uniformity of good tea, such as they best like, by attending to the principle of making it—that is to say, to time, and quantities, and temperature. There is no other mystery in the teapot.

Tea made in the kettle. Where there are no cups or teapot put the leaves in the pot or kettle, and drink through a reed with a wisp of grass in it, as they do in Paraguay. If there are cups and no teapot, the leaves may be put into the pot, previously enclosed in a loose gauze or muslin bag to prevent their floating about. A contrivance is sold in the shops for this purpose; it is made of metal gauze, and shaped like an egg. A purse made of metal rings would be better, for it would pack flat; but the advantage of muslin over metal apparatus is that you may throw away bag and all, and avoid the trouble of cleaning.

Tea made overnight. To prepare tea for a very early breakfast, make it overnight, and pour it away from the tea leaves into another vessel. It will keep perfectly well, for it is by long standing with the tea leaves that it becomes bitter. In the morning, simply warm it up. Tea is drunk at a temperature of 140° Fahr., or 90° above an average night temperature of 50°. It is more than twice as easy to raise the temperature up to 140° than to 212°, letting alone the trouble of teamaking.

Sir Samuel Baker (British, 1821-93) advanced the spread of Empire with forays in Ceylon (1848) and central Africa (1861-65 and 1869-74). He was knighted for his contributions yet was never fully accepted by Victorian society, in part because he bought his second wife at a white slave auction in Vidin, Bulgaria and, despite traveling with her extensively in Africa, never legally married her. Baker was an accomplished hunter, which he once demonstrated to friends by tracking and killing a deer with only a knife and his wits.

Thomas Witlam Atkinson
(British, 1799-1861) was an
architect and illustrator who,
with his wife Lucy, traveled
throughout the borderland
territory between Russia and
China. He was the author
of several books on Siberia,
Mongolia, and other parts of
central Asia.

Tea and coffee, without hot water. In Unyoro, Sir
S. Baker◆ says, they have no idea of using coffee
as a drink, but simply chew it raw as a stimulant.
In Chinese Tartary, travelers who have no means
of making a cup of tea will chew the leaves as a substitute. Mr. Atkinson◆ told me how very grateful he
had found this makeshift.

FIREPLACES FOR COOKING.

The most elementary fireplace consists of three
stones in a triangle, to support the pot. If stones are
not procurable, three piles of mud, or three stakes of
green wood driven into the earth, are an equivalent.
Small recesses neatly cut in a bank, one for each
fireplace, are much used when the fuel is dry and
well prepared. A more elaborate plan is to excavate a
shallow saucer-like hole in the ground, a foot or 18
inches in diameter, and kneading the soil so exca-
vated into a circular wall, with a
doorway in the windward side:
the upper surface is curved, so
as to leave three pointed turrets,
upon which the cooking vessel
rests, as in the sketch. Thus the
wind enters at the doorway,
and the flames issue through the curved depressions
at the top and lick round the cooking vessel placed
above. The wall is sometimes built of stones.

Trenches and holes. In cooking for a large party
with a small supply of fuel, either dig a narrow
trench, above which all the pots and kettles may
stand in a row, and in which the fire is made—the
mouth being open to the wind, and a small chim-

ney built at the other end; or else dig a round hole, one foot deep, and place the pots in a ring on its edge, half resting on the earth and half overlapping the hole. A space will remain in the middle of them, and through this the fire must be fed.

Eskimo lamp. The cooking of the Eskimo is wholly effected by stone lamps with wicks made of moss, which are so carefully arranged that the flame gives little or no smoke. Their lamps vary in size from 6 to 18 inches. Each of the bits of moss gives a small but very bright flame. This lamp is all in all to the Eskimo; it dries their clothes and melts the snow for their drinking water; its construction is very ingenious; without it they could not have inhabited the Arctic regions.

OVENS.

Bedouin oven. Dig a hole in the ground; wall and roof it with stones, leaving small apertures in the top. Then make a roaring fire in and about the oven (the roof having been temporarily removed for the purpose), and when the stones (including those of the roof) have become very hot, sweep away the ashes and strew the inside of the oven with grass, or leaves, taking care that whatever is used has no disagreeable taste, else it would be communicated to the flesh. Then put in the meat: it is a common plan to sew it up in its own skin, which shields it from dust and at the same time retains its juices from evaporating. Now replace the roof, a matter of some difficulty on account of the stones being hot, and therefore requiring previous rehearsal. Lastly, rake the fire again over the oven and let the baking

☞ The ruder tribes of the Indian Archipelago use a bamboo to boil their rice: "The green cane resisting the fire sufficiently long for the cooking of one mass of rice." (Crawfurd.)

☞ Where there are no stones of which ovens may be built, and where there are old white-ant hills, the natives commonly dig holes in the sides of the ant hills and use them for that purpose.

continue for some hours. An entire sheep can be baked easily in this way. The same process is used for baking vegetables, except with the addition of pouring occasionally boiling water upon them through the roof.

Gold digger's oven. The figure represents a section of the oven. A hole or deep notch is dug into the side of a bank and two flat stones are slid horizontally, like shelves, into grooves made in the sides of the hole, as shown in the figure; where it will be observed that the uppermost stone does not quite reach to the face of the bank, and that the lowermost stone does not quite reach to the back of the hole. A fire of red-hot embers is placed on the floor of the hole and the bread about to be baked is laid upon the lowermost stone. Lastly, another flat stone is used to close the mouth of the oven: it is set with its edge on the floor of the hole: it leans forward with the middle of its face resting against the front edge of the lowermost stone, a narrow interval being left between its top and the edge of the uppermost stone. This interval serves as a vent to the hot air from the embers, which takes the course shown in the figure. The oven should be thoroughly heated before the bread is put in.

Baking between two stones. For baking slices of meat or thin cakes, it is sufficient to lay one large stone above another with a few pebbles between, to

☞ A book on cooking is of no use at all in the rougher kinds of travel, for all its recipes consist of phrases such as, "Take a pound of so-and-so, half a pound of something else, a pinch of this, and a handful of that." Now in the bush a man has probably none of these things—he certainly has not all of them—and, therefore, the recipe is worthless.

prevent them from touching. Next make a large fire about the stones until they are thoroughly hot; then sweep away the embers and insert the slices.

Clay ovens. I have heard of a very neat construction, built with clay in which grass had been kneaded. A fire was lit inside to dry the work as it progressed, while the builder placed rings of clay in tiers one above the other, until a complete dome was made without mold or framework. Time was allowed for each ring to dry sufficiently before the next one was added.

Baking beneath a campfire. A small piece of meat, enough for four or five people, can be baked by simply scraping a tolerably deep hole under the bivouac fire; putting in the meat rolled in the skin to which it is attached, and covering it with earth and fire. It is a slow process of cooking, for it requires many hours; but the meat, when done, is soft and juicy, and the skin gelatinous and excellent.

Baking in pots. A capital oven is improvised by means of two earthen or metal cooking pots, of which one is placed on the fire, and in it the article to be baked; the other pot is put upon its top, as a cover, and in it a shovelful of red-hot embers.

☞ It is easy to replace a lost spoon by cutting a new one out of hard wood, or by making one of horn.

☞ Each of the men on a riding expedition should carry his own tin mug, either tied to his waist or to his saddle. A wooden bowl is the best vessel for tea, and even for soup, if you have means of frequently washing it: tin mugs burn the lips too much. Wooden bowls are always used in Tibet; they are cut out of the knots that are found in timber.

SHOOTING GAME.

NOCTURNAL ANIMALS.

SCARECROWS.

PAN-HUNTING.

CHARGING ANIMALS.

DOGS KEPT AT BAY.

HIDING GAME.

DIVISION OF GAME.

DUCK SHOOTING.

CROCODILE SHOOTING.

TRACKS.

CAPTURING GAME.

CATCHING WITH THE HAND.

BOLAS.

☞ "Look at the gun, but never let the gun look at you, or at your companions," is a golden rule; for among the chances of death to which a traveler is exposed, that of being shot by an attendant's gun going off accidentally ranks high.

GAME

SHOOTING GAME.

American bushrangers advocate a long heavy pea–rifle, on the plea of its accurate shooting, and the enormous saving in weight of ammunition when bullets of a small size are used. The objections to small-bored rifles are, insufficiency against large game (even with conical bullets), and a tendency to become foul after a few shots. A short light rifle, whether with a large or a small bore, is, I believe, utterly worthless. In the hands of a man trembling with running and with exhaustion, it shakes like a wand: the shorter the rifle, the more quickly does it oscillate, and of course, in the same proportion, is it difficult to catch the exact moment when the sights cover the object.

For the larger kinds of game, such as elephants and buffaloes, experienced sportsmen mostly prefer guns of immense bore, carrying round bullets that weigh a quarter of a pound. The recoil is tremendous, and would injure the shoulder if the sportsman did not use a pad against which he rests the gun. The guns must be strong because very large charges of powder are invariably used where great power of penetration is required. African sportsmen found this out experimentally long before the idea occurred to artillerists.

NOCTURNAL ANIMALS.

There are a large number of night-feeding animals upon whose flesh a traveler might easily support himself, but of whose existence he would have few indications by daylight observation only. The following remarks of Professor Owen in respect to Australia are very suggestive:

> *All the marsupial animals—and it is one of their curious peculiarities—are nocturnal. Even the kangaroo, which is the least so, is scarcely ever seen feeding out on the plains in broad daylight: it prefers the early morning dawn, or the short twilight; and, above all, the bright moonlight nights. With regard to most of the other Australian forms of marsupial animals, they are most strictly nocturnal; so that, if a traveler were not aware of that peculiarity, he might fancy himself traversing a country destitute of the mammalian grade of animal life. If, however, after a weary day's journey, he could be awakened, and were to look out about the moonlight glade or scrub, or if he were to set traps by night, he would probably be surprised to find how great a number of interesting forms of mammalian animals were to be met with, in places where there was not the slightest appearance of them in the daytime.*

SCARECROWS.

A string with feathers tied to it at intervals, like the tail of a boy's kite, will scare most animals of the deer tribe, by their fluttering; and, in want of a sufficient force of men, passes may be closed by this contrivance. The Swedes use "lappar," viz. pieces of canvas of half the height of a man, painted in glaring colors and left to flutter from a line.

Mr. Lloyd tells us of a peasant who, when walking without a gun, saw a glutton up in a tree. He at once took off his hat and coat and rigged out a scarecrow, the counterpart of himself, which he fixed close by, for the purpose of frightening the beast from coming down; he then went leisurely home to fetch his gun: this notable expedient succeeded perfectly.

STALKING-HORSES.

Artificial. A stalking-horse, or cow, is made by cutting out a piece of strong canvas into the shape of the animal and painting it properly. Loops are sewn in different places, through which sticks are passed to stretch the curves into shape: a stake planted in the ground serves as a buttress to support the apparatus: at a proper height there is a loophole to fire through. It packs up into a roll of canvas and a bundle of five or six sticks. Bushes are used much in the same way. Colonel Hawker◆ made a contrivance upon wheels which he pushed before him. The Eskimo shoot seals by pushing a white screen before them over the ice on a sledge. (Kane.)

Colonel Peter Hawker (British, 1786-1853) was an avid hunter and author of the seminal *Instructions to Young Sportsmen in All that Relates to Guns and Shooting* (1814).

Real. Both horses and oxen can be trained to shield a sportsman: they are said to enter into the spirit of the thing, and to show wonderful craft, walking round and round the object in narrowing circles, and stopping to graze unconcernedly on witnessing the least sign of alarm. Oxen are taught to obey a touch on the horn: the common but cruel way of training them is to hammer and batter the horns for hours together and on many days successively: they then become inflamed at the root and are highly sensitive.

PAN HUNTING (USED AT SALT LICKS).

Pan hunting is a method of hunting deer at night. An iron pan attached to a long stick, serving as a handle, is carried in the left hand over the left shoulder; near where the hand grasps the handle, is a small projecting stick, forming a fork on which to rest the rifle, when firing. The pan is filled with burning pine knots, which, being saturated with turpentine, shed a brilliant and constant light all around; shining into the eyes of any deer that may come in that direction, and making them look like two balls of fire. The effect is most curious to those unaccustomed to it. The distance between the eyes of the deer as he approaches, appears gradually to increase, reminding one of the lamps of a traveling carriage. (Palliser. ◈)

CHARGING ANIMALS.

The rush of an enraged animal is far more easily avoided than is usually supposed. The way the Spanish bullfighters play with the bull is well known: any man can avoid a mere headlong charge. Even the speed of a racer, which is undeniably far greater than any wild quadruped, does not exceed 30 miles an hour or four times the speed of a man. The speed of an ordinary horse is not more than 24 miles an hour: now even the fastest wild beast is unable to catch an ordinary horse, except by crawling unobserved close to his side and springing upon him; therefore I am convinced that the rush of no wild animal exceeds 24 miles an hour, or three times the speed of a man.

Unthinking persons talk of the fearful rapidity of a lion or tiger's spring. It is not rapid at all: it is a slow movement, as must be evident from the following consideration. No wild animal can leap ten yards, and they all make a high trajectory in their leaps. Now, think of the speed of a ball thrown, or rather pitched, with just sufficient force to be caught by a person ten yards off: it is a mere nothing. The catcher can play with it as he likes; he has even time to turn after it, if thrown wide. But the speed of a springing animal is undeniably the same as that of a ball, thrown so as to make a flight

Captain John Palliser (British, 1817-1887), an Irish geographer and explorer, led a scientific expedition through western Canada, from the Red River Colony to the Pacific, from 1857 to 1860. Commissioned by the British to gather information on the resources of the territory, his company returned with reports of fertile lands and an abundance of game which enticed settlers to follow.

☞ It is perfectly easy, for a person who is cool, to avoid an animal by dodging to one side or other of a bush. Few animals turn if the rush be unsuccessful. The buffalo is an exception; he regularly hunts a man and is therefore peculiarly dangerous.

of equal length and height in the air. The corollary to all this is that, if charged, you must keep cool and watchful, and your chance of escape is far greater than non-sportsmen would imagine. The blow of the free paw is far swifter than the bound.

DOGS KEPT AT BAY.

A correspondent assures me that "a dog flying at a man may be successfully repelled by means of a stout stick held horizontally, a hand at each end, and used to thrust the dog backwards over, by meeting him across the throat or breast. If followed by a blow on the nose as the brute is falling, the result will be sooner attained."

HIDING GAME.

In hiding game from birds of prey, bush it over, and they will seldom find it out; birds cannot smell well, but they have keen eyes. The meat should be hung from an overhanging bough; then, if the birds find it out, there will be no place for them to stand on and tear it. Leaving a handkerchief or a shirt to flutter from a tree will scare animals of prey for a short time.

DIVISION OF GAME.

It is a very general and convenient rule (though, like all fixed rules, often unfair) that the animal should belong to the man who first wounded him, however slight the wound might have been; but that he or they who actually killed the animal should have a right to a slice of the meat: it must, however, be understood that the man who gave the first wound should not thenceforward withdraw from

☞ A watchdog usually desists from flying at a stranger when he seats himself quietly on the ground, like Ulysses. The dog then contents himself with barking and keeping guard until his master arrives.

the chase; if he does so, his claim is lost. In America the skin belongs to the first shot, the carcass is divided equally among the whole party. Whaling crews are bound by similar customs, in which nice distinctions are made, and which have all the force of laws.

DUCK SHOOTING.

Wooden ducks, ballasted with lead and painted, may be used at night as decoy ducks; or the skins of birds already shot may be stuffed and employed for the same purpose. They should be anchored in the water, or made fast to a frame attached to the shooting punt, and dressed with sedge. If real ducks be used as decoy birds, the males should be tied in one place and the females in another to induce them to quack. An artificial island may be made to attract ducks when there is no real one.

☞ It is convenient to sink a large barrel into the flat marsh or mud, as a dry place to stand or sit in, when waiting for the birds to come. A lady suggests to me that if the sportsman took a bottle of hot water to put under his feet, it would be a great comfort to him, and in this I quite agree; I would take a keg of hot water, when about it.

CROCODILE SHOOTING.

Mr. Gilby says, speaking of Egypt:

I killed several crocodiles by digging pits on the sand-islands and sleeping a part of the night in them; a dry shred of palm branch, the color of the sand, round the hole, formed a screen to put the gun through. Their flesh was most excellent eating—half-way between meat and fish: I had it several times. The difficulty of shooting them was, that the falcons and spurwing plovers would hover round the pit, when the crocodiles invariably took to the water. Their sight and hearing were good, but their scent indifferent. I generally got a shot or two at daybreak after sleeping in the pit.

TRACKS.

When the neighborhood of a drinking place is trodden down with tracks, "describe a circle a little distance from it, to ascertain if it be much

☞ It is related in the *Apocrypha* that the prophet Daniel sprinkled sand on the ground when he wished to learn who it really was who every night consumed the meat which was placed before the idol of Bel, and which the idol itself was supposed to eat: he thus discovered that the priests and their families had a secret door by which they entered the temple, and convinced the king of the matter by showing him their footprints.

The whole species of man yields a powerful and wide-spreading emanation that is utterly disgusting and repulsive to every animal in its wild state

frequented. This is the manner in which spoor should at all times be sought for." (Cumming's *Life in South Africa*.) To know if a burrow be tenanted, go to work on the same principle, but if the ground be hard, sprinkle sand over it in order to show the tracks more clearly.

CAPTURING GAME.

A trapper will never succeed unless he thoroughly enters into the habits of life and mind of wild animals. He must ever bear in mind how suspicious they are; how quickly their eye is caught by unusual traces; and, lastly, how strong and enduring a taint is left by the human touch. Our own senses do not make us aware of what it is disagreeable enough to acknowledge, that the whole species of man yields a powerful and wide-spreading emanation that is utterly disgusting and repulsive to every animal in its wild state.

It requires some experience to realize this fact: a man must frequently have watched the heads of a herd of far-distant animals tossed up in alarm the moment that they catch his wind; he must have observed the tracks of animals—how, when they crossed his path of the preceding day, the beast that made the tracks has stopped, scrutinized, and shunned it—before he can believe what a Yahoo he is among the brute creation. No cleanliness of the individual seems to diminish this remarkable odor: indeed, the more civilized the man, the more subtle does it appear to be; the touch of a gamekeeper scares less than that of the master, and the touch of a negro or bushman less than that of a traveler from Europe.

If a novice thinks he will trap successfully by such artless endeavors as putting a bait on the plate of a trap that is covered over with moss, or by digging a pitfall in the middle of a wild beast's track, he is utterly mistaken. The bait should be thrown on the ground and the trap placed on the way to it; then the animal's mind, being fixed on the meat, takes less heed of the footpath. Or a pitfall should be made near the main path; this being subsequently stopped by boughs causes the animal to walk in the bushes and to tumble into the covered hole.

☞ After setting traps, Mr. St. John recommends the use of a small branch of a tree; first, to smooth the ground, and then, having dipped it in water, to sprinkle the place: this entirely obliterates all footmarks.

Springes. Harden the wood of which the mechanism has to be made by means of fire; either baking it in hot sand or ashes, or otherwise applying heat to a degree just short of charring its surface. The mechanism will then retain the sharpness of its edges under a continuance of pressure and during many hours of wet weather. The slighter the strain on the springe, the more delicately can its mechanism be set.

Nooses. Catgut makes better nooses than string because it is stiff enough to keep in shape when set. Brass wire that has been heated red-hot is excellent, for it has no tendency whatever to twist and yet is perfectly pliable. Fish hooks are sometimes attached to springes; sometimes a tree is bent down and a strong cord is used for the noose, by which large animals are strangled up in the air, as leopards are in Abyssinia. A noose may be set in any place where there is a run; it can be kept spread out by thin rushes or twigs set crosswise in it. If the animal it is set for can gnaw, a heavy stone should be loosely

☞ It is a very convenient plan for a traveler who has not time to look for runs, to make little hedges across a creek, or at right angles to a clump of trees, and to set his snares in gaps left in these artificial hedges. On the same principle, artificial islands of piles and faggots are commonly made in lakes that are destitute of any real ones, in order that they may become a resort of wildfowl.

Roualeyn George Gordon Cumming (British, 1820-1866) was an immense man of great physical strength possessed by a passion for hunting. During a five-year sojourn in South Africa he was said to have shot at least one of each species of fauna. He became known as The Lion Hunter (in a kilt) and wrote *A Hunter's Life in South Africa,* widely reprinted for years. After exhibiting his trophies in England, he showed his collection in his own permanent museum in Scotland.

☞ It is difficult to prevent the covers of pitfalls becoming hollow: the only way is to build the roofs in somewhat of an arch so as to allow room for subsidence.

☞ If a herd of animals be driven over pitfalls, some are sure to be pushed in, as the crush makes it impossible for the beasts, however wary, to pick their way.

propped up which the animal in its struggles may set free, and by the weight of which it may be hung up and strangled.

Javelins. Heavy poisoned javelins, hung over elephant and hippopotamus paths and dropped on a catch being touched, after the manner of a springe, are used generally in Africa. They sometimes are a

> *sharp little assegai, or spike, most thoroughly poisoned, and stuck firmly into the end of a heavy block of thornwood, about four feet long and five inches in diameter. This formidable affair is suspended over the centre of a sea-cow path, at about thirty feet from the ground, by a bark cord, which passes over a high branch of a tree, and thence, by a peg, on one side of a path beneath.* (Gordon Cumming.◈)

Pitfalls. Very small pitfalls, with sharpened stakes planted inside them, that have been baked hard by the fire and well poisoned, are easily to be set, but they are very dangerous to man and beast. In preparing a pitfall for animals of prey, it is usual to ascertain whether they are deep enough by putting in a large dog; if he cannot get out, it is very unlikely that any wild beast can.

Pitfalls are often dug in great numbers near frequented watering places to which numerous intersecting paths lead. By stopping up particular paths, the pitfalls can be brought separately into use; therefore, those pitfalls need never be employed in which animals have been freshly killed, and where the smell of blood would scare the game.

Traps. Steel traps should never be tied fast or the captured animal may struggle loose, or even gnaw off his leg. It is best to cut small bushes, and merely to secure the traps to their cut ends. Steel traps are of but little use to a traveler.

Hawks are trapped by selecting a bare tree that stands in an open space: its top is sawn off level and a trap is put upon it: the bait is laid somewhere near, on the ground: the bird is sure to visit the pole, either before or after he has fed.

Poison. Savages frequently poison the water of drinking places and follow, capture, and eat the poisoned animals. Nux vomica or strychnine is a very dangerous poison to use, but it affords the best means of ridding a neighborhood of noxious beasts and birds: if employed to kill beasts, put it in the belly; if, birds, in the eye, of the bait. Meat for killing beasts should be set after nightfall, else the crows and other birds will be sure to find it out and eat it up before the beasts have time to discover it. It would be unsafe to eat an animal killed with strychnine on account of the deadliness of the poison.

CATCHING WITH THE HAND.

Ducks. We hear of Hindus who, taking advantage of the many gourds floating on their waters, put one of them on their heads and wade in among wild ducks; they pull them down, one after another, by their legs, under water, wring their necks, and tie them to their girdle. But in Australia, a swimmer binds grass and rushes, or weeds, round his head and takes a long fishing rod with a slip noose working over the pliant twig that forms the last joint of the rod. When he comes near, he gently raises the end and, putting the noose over the head of the bird, draws it under water to him. He thus catches one after another, and tucks the caught ones in his belt.

☞ The Swedes put fulminating powder in a raw shankbone and throw it down to the wolves; when one of these gnaws and crunches it, it blows his head to atoms.

☞ Arrows are most readily poisoned by steeping a thread in the juice and wrapping it round the barbs. Serpents' venom may always be used with effect.

☞ It is useless that I should enter into details about making and wielding the lasso, for it is impossible to become moderately adept in its use without months of instruction and practice.

A windy day is generally chosen because the water is ruffled. (Eyre. ◈)

Condors and vultures are caught by spreading a raw oxhide under which a man creeps, with a piece of string in his hand, while one or two other men are posted in ambush close by to give assistance at the proper moment. When the bird flies down upon the bait, his legs are seized by the man underneath the skin and are tied within it, as in a bag. All his flapping is then useless; he cannot do mischief with his claws and he is easily overpowered.

BOLAS.

The bolas consists of three balls, either of lead or stone; two of them are heavy but the third is rather lighter: they are fastened to long elastic strings, made of twisted sinews, and the ends of the strings are all tied together. The Indian holds the lightest of the three balls in his hand, and swings the two others in a wide circle above his head; then taking his aim, at the distance of about fifteen or twenty paces, he lets go the hand-ball; all the three balls whirl in a circle and twine round the object aimed at. The aim is usually taken at the hind legs of the animals and, the cords twisting round them, they become firmly bound. It requires great skill and long practice to throw the bolas dexterously, especially when on horseback. A novice in the art incurs the risk of dangerously hurting either himself or his horse by not giving the balls the proper swing, or by letting go the hand-ball too soon. (Tschudi's◈ *Peru.*)

Edward John Eyre (British, 1815-1901) went to Australia at the age of seventeen; at twenty-four he explored a 1,000-mile route in southwestern Australia with an aboriginal friend named Wylie. At times they lived on kangaroos and, for water, sucked the roots of gum trees. In later life Eyre was lieutenant governor of New Zealand and governor of various Caribbean islands, including Jamaica.

Johann Jakob von Tschudi (Swiss, 1818-1889) was a naturalist who explored parts of South America, primarily Peru and Brazil, and published many books on his findings. He later became the Swiss ambassador to Brazil.

FISHING

FISHING TACKLE.

A traveler should always take a few hooks with him. They should be of the very small and also of the middling-sized sorts; he might have a dozen of each sort whipped onto gut, and at least a couple of casting lines with which to use them; also several dozens of tinned iron fishhooks of various sizes, such as are used at sea; and plenty of line.

Fishing lines. Twisted sinews will make a fishing line. To make a strong fine line, unravel a good silk handkerchief and twist the threads into a whipcord. Gut is made from silkworms, but the scrapings of the membrane in the manufacture of catgut make a fine, strong, and somewhat transparent thread.

Reel. If you have no reel, make a couple of gimlet holes, 6 inches apart, in the butt of your rod at the place where the reel is usually clamped; drive wooden pegs into these, and wind your spare line round them, as in fig. 1. The pegs should not be quite square with the butt, but should slope a little, each away from the other, that the line may be better retained on them. A long line is conveniently wound on a square frame, as shown in the annexed sketch *(fig. 2)*; and a shorter line, as in fig. 3.

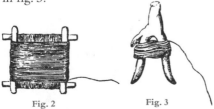

Fig. 2   Fig. 3

FISHING TACKLE.

BOAT FISHING..

NETS.

SPEARING FISH.

OTTERS, CORMORANTS AND DOGS.

☞ To recover a lost line: make a drag of a small bushy tree with plenty of branches that are so lopped off as to leave spikes on the trunk. This is to be weighted with a stone and dragged along the bottom.

Fig. 1

☞ If you have no equivalent for a reel, and if your tackle is slight and the fish likely to be large, provide yourself with a bladder or other float; tie it to the line, and cast the whole adrift.

BOAT FISHING.

In fishing with a long ground-line and many hooks, it is of importance to avoid entanglements; make a box in which to coil the line, and a great many deep saw cuts across the sides into which the thin short lines, to which the hooks are whipped, may be jammed.

Fishermen who do not use oars, but paddles, tie a loop to their line: they put their thumb through the loop and fish while they paddle.

NETS.

A small square net may be best turned to account by sinking it in holes and other parts of a river which fish frequent; throwing in bait to attract them over it; and then hauling up suddenly. The arrangement shown in the figure is very common. A seine net may be furnished with bladder for floats, or else with pieces of light wood charred to make them more buoyant. The hauling-ropes may be made of bark steeped for

☞ To see things deep under water, such as dead seals, use a long box or tube with a piece of glass at the lower end; this removes entirely the glare of the water and the effects of a rippled surface. Mr. Campbell, of Islay, suggests that a small glass window might be let into the bottom of the boat: plate-glass would be amply strong enough.

three weeks, till the inner bark separates from the outer when the latter is twisted into a rope. (Lloyd.) Wherever small fish are swimming in shoals near the surface, there the water is sure to be rippled.

SPEARING FISH.

The weapon used is identical with Neptune's or Britannia's trident, only the prongs should be more numerous and be placed nearer together in order to catch small fish: the length of the handle gives steadiness to the blow. In spearing by torch-light, a broad oval piece of bark is coated with wet mud and in it a blazing fire is lighted. It is fixed on a stage, or it is held in the bow of the boat, so high as to be above the spearman's eyes. He can see everything by its light, especially if the water be not above 4 feet deep and the bottom sandy. But there are not many kinds of wood that will burn with a sufficiently bright flame; the dry bark of some resinous tree is often used. If tarred rope can be obtained, it may simply be wound round a pole fixed in the bow of the boat and lighted. Fish can also be shot with a bow and a barbed arrow to which a string is attached.

OTTERS, CORMORANTS, AND DOGS.

Both otters and cormorants are trained to catch fish for their masters, and dogs are trained by the Patagonians to drive fish into the nets and to frighten them from breaking loose when the net is being hauled in. Cormorants in China fish during the winter from October to May, working from 10 A.M. to 5 P.M., at which hour their dinner is given to them. When they fish, a straw tie is put round their necks to keep them from swallowing the fish, but not so tight as to slip down and choke them. A boat takes out ten or twelve of these birds. They obey the voice: if they are disobedient, the water near them is struck with the back of the oar. As soon as one of them has caught a fish he is called to the boat, and the oar is held out for him to step upon.

☞ Lime thrown into a pond will kill the fish; and the similar but far more energetic properties of *Cocculus indicus* are well known. Throughout tropical Africa and in South America, the natives catch fish by poisoning them. Dams are made which, when the river is very low, enclose deep pools of water with no current; into these the poison is thrown: it intoxicates the fish, which float and are taken by the hand.

☞ It requires caution to train a cormorant because the bird has a habit, when angry, of striking with its beak at its instructor's eye with an exceedingly rapid and sure stroke.

FUEL.

SMALL FUEL FOR LIGHTING
THE FIRE.

TO KINDLE A SPARK INTO
A FLAME.

CAMPFIRES.

FIREPLACES IN BOATS.

FIRES IN THE EARLY MORNING.

FIRE

Although, in the teeth of every precaution, fires constantly break out, yet when a traveler wants a light and does not happen to have any of his ingenious fire-making contrivances at hand, it is very difficult for him to obtain it. And further, though sparks of their own accord and in the most unlikely places too often give rise to conflagrations, yet it requires much skill and practice to succeed without fail in coaxing a small spark into a serviceable camp fire. Therefore every traveler should carry on his person the means of procuring a light under ordinary circumstances of wind and weather; that is to say, he should have in his pocket a light handy steel, a flint or an agate, and amadou or other tinder.

FUEL.

Firewood. There is a knack in finding firewood. It should be looked for under bushes; the stump of a tree that is rotted nearly to the ground has often a magnificent root fit to blaze throughout the night.

Dry cattle dung. The dry dung of cattle and other animals, as found on the ground, is very generally used throughout the world in default of better fuel, and there is nothing whatever objectionable in employing it. The Canadians call it by the apt name of "bois de vache." In North and South Africa it is frequently used; throughout a large part of Armenia and of Tibet the natives rely entirely upon it. There is a great convenience in this sort of fuel because, as it is only in camps that fuel is wanted, so it is precisely at old encamping places that cattle dung is abundantly found.

Bones. Another remarkable substitute for firewood is bones, a fact which Mr. Darwin was, I believe, the first to mention. The bones of an animal, when freshly killed, make good fuel, and even those of cooked meat, and such as have been exposed to the air for some days, will greatly increase the heat of a scanty fire. Their smell is not disagreeable: it is simply that of roast or burnt meat. In the Falkland Islands, where firewood is scarce, it is not unusual to cook part of the meat of a slaughtered bull with its own bones. When the fire is once started with a few sticks, it burns well and hotly. The flame of course depends on the fat within the bones, and therefore the fatter the animal the better the fire.

Seaweed makes a hot though not a cheerful fire. It is largely used. The vraic or seaweed gatherers of the Channel Islands are represented in many picturesque sketches. The weed is carted home, spread out, and dried.

Peat. Travelers must bear in mind that peat will burn, especially as the countries in which it is found are commonly destitute of firewood and, besides that, are marshy, cold, and aguish.

Charcoal is frequently carried by travelers in sacks; they use a prepared charcoal in the East, which is made in the form of very large buttons that are carried strung together on a string. An Indian correspondent informs me that they are made by mixing powdered charcoal with molasses in the

☞ During the Russian campaign in 1829, the troops suffered so severely from cold at Adrianople that the cemeteries were ransacked for bones for fuel. (Moltke.)

proportion of ten to one or thereabouts, rolling the mass into balls, and drying them in the sun. A single ball is called a "gul." They are used for igniting hookahs: they are also burnt inside the smoothing-iron used by washermen in order to heat it. The juice or sap of many plants would probably answer the purpose of molasses in their preparation.

SMALL FUEL FOR LIGHTING THE FIRE.

Shreds and fibers. The live spark has to be received, and partly enclosed, in a loose heap or "nest" of finely shredded fuel. The substances for making such a nest are one or other of the following list: dry grass of the finest kinds; leaves; moss; lichen, and wild cotton; stalks or bark, broken up and rubbed small between the fingers; peat or cattle-dung pulverized; paper that has been doubled up in many folds and then cut with a sharp knife into the finest possible shavings; tow, or what is the same thing, oakum, made by unraveling rope or string; and scrapings and fine shavings from a log of wood. The shreds that are intended to touch the live spark should be reduced to the finest fiber; the outside of the nest may be of coarser, but still somewhat delicate, material.

Small sticks. There should be abundance of small sticks, and if neither these nor any equivalent for them are to be picked up, the traveler should split up his larger firewood with his knife in order to make them. It is a wise economy of time and patience to prepare plenty of these; otherwise it will occasionally happen that the whole stock will be consumed and no fire made. Then the traveler must recommence the work from the very beginning, under the disadvantage of increasing darkness. I have made many experiments myself, and have seen many novices as well as old campaigners try to make fires, and have concluded that, to ensure success, the traveler should be provided with small bundles of sticks of each of the following sizes:

1st, size of lucifer match;

2nd, of lead pencil;

3rd, smaller than little finger;

4th, size of forefinger;

5th, stout stakes.

In wet weather, the most likely places to find wherewithal to light a fire are under large stones and other shelter; but in soaking wet weather, little chips of dry wood can hardly be procured except by cutting them with an axe out of the middle of a log. The fire may then be begun, as the late Admiral the Hon. C. Murray◈ well recommended in his travels in North America, in the frying pan itself, for want of a dry piece of ground.

TO KINDLE A SPARK INTO A FLAME.

By whirling.

1st. Arrange the fuel into logs; into small fuel, assorted as described above, and into shreds and fibres.

2nd. Make a loose nest of the fiber, just like a sparrow's nest in shape and size, and let the finer part of the fibers be inwards.

3rd. Drop the lighted tinder in the nest.

4th. Holding the nest quite loosely in the half-closed hand, whirl the outstretched arm in vertical circles round the shoulder joint, as indicated by the dotted

As a young lord from the Scottish House of Dunsmore, **Charles Augustus Murray** (British, 1806–1895) traveled in North America, camping for several months with a Pawnee tribe. In upstate New York he fell in love with an American beauty, Elsie Wadsworth, but her father forbade their marriage. Murray poured his heartaches into a romantic novel, *The Prairie Bird* (1844). When Wadsworth's father died the couple reunited and married in Westminster Abbey, fifteen years after their courtship began. At that time Murray was consul-general in Egypt, and during their honeymoon there he ordered a servant to inscribe his bride's name in the rock at the entry to Ramses II's Temple of Abu Simbel. (The graffito remains legible today.) Sadly, Elsie died in childbirth a year later.

line in the diagram. In 30 seconds, or about 40 revo-
lutions, it will begin to glow, and will shortly after
burst out in a grand flame.

5th. Drop it, and pile small twigs round it, and nurse
the young fire carefully, bearing in mind the proverb
that "small sticks kindle a flame, but large ones put
it out."

By blowing. Savages usually kindle the flame by
blowing at the live spark and feeding it with little
bits of stick, just so much as is necessary. But it is
difficult to acquire the art of doing this well, and I
decidedly recommend the plan I have described in
the foregoing paragraph, in preference to it. When
the wind blows steadily and freshly, it suffices to
hold up the "nest" against the wind.

Sulfur matches are so very useful to convert a
spark into a flame, and they are so easily made, in
any quantity, out of split wood, straws, &c., if the
traveler will only take the trouble of carrying a small
lump of sulfur in his baggage, that they always ought
to be at hand. The sulfur is melted on a heated
stone, or in an old spoon, bit of crockery, bit of tin
with a dent made in it, or even a piece of paper,
and the points of the pieces of wood dipped in the
molten mass. A small chip of sulfur pushed into the
cleft end of a splinter of wood makes a fair substitute for a match.

CAMPFIRES.

Large logs. The principle of making large logs
to burn brightly is to allow air to reach them on all
sides, and yet to place them so closely together that
each supports the combustion of the rest. A com-

*Small sticks
kindle a flame,
but large ones
put it out*

mon plan is to make the fire with three logs whose ends cross each other, as in the diagram. The dots represent the extent of the fire. As the ends burn away, the logs are pushed closer together. Another plan is to lay the logs parallel with the burning ends to the windward, then they continue burning together.

In the pine forests of the North, at winter time, it is usual to fell a large tree and, cutting a piece 6 or 8 feet long off the large end, to lay the thick short piece upon the long one, which is left lying on the ground, having previously cut flat with the axe the sides that come in contact, and notched them so as to make the upper log lie steady. The chips are then heaped in between the logs and are set fire to; the flame runs in between them and the heat of each log helps the other to burn. It is the work of nearly an hour to prepare such a fire, but when made, it lasts throughout the night.

☞ In all cases, one or two great logs are far better than many small ones, as these burn fast away and require constant looking after.

Brushwood. If in a country where only a number of small sticks and no large logs can be collected as firewood, the best plan is to encamp after the manner of the Ovampos. These, as they travel, collect sticks, each man his own faggot, and when they stop, each takes eight or nine stones as large as bricks or larger, and sets them in a circle, and within these he lights up his little fire. Now the party make their fireplaces close together, in two or more parallel lines, and sleep in between them. The stones prevent the embers from flying about and doing mischief, and also, after the fires have quite burnt out, they continue to radiate heat.

☞ Many serious accidents occur from a large log burning away and toppling over with a crash, sending a volley of blazing cinders among the sleeping party.

FIREPLACES IN BOATS.

In boating excursions, daub a lump of clay on the bottom of the boat, beneath the fireplace—it will secure the timbers from fire. "Our primitive kitchen was a square wooden box, lined with clay and filled with sand, upon which three or four large stones were placed to form a hearth." (Burton's *Medinah*.)

FIRES IN THE EARLY MORNING.

Should your stock of fuel consist of large logs and but little brushwood, keep all you can spare of the latter to make a blaze, when you get up to catch and pack the cattle in the dark and early morning. As you travel on, if it be bitter cold, carry a firebrand in your hand, near your mouth, as a respirator—it is very comforting; then, when the fire of it burns dull, thrust the brand for a few moments in any tuft of dry grass you may happen to pass by, which will blaze up and give a new life to the brand.

☞ If charcoal be carried, a small chafing dish, or other substitute for a fireplace, ought also to be taken, together with a set of tin cooking utensils.

☞ On very deep snow, a hearth has to be made of a number of green logs, upon which the fire may be made.

BEDDING

MATTRESSES AND THEIR
SUBSTITUTES.

PREPARING THE GROUND FOR
A BED.

COVERLETS.

SLEEPING BAGS.

It is a common idea among men who are preparing to travel for the first time, that all the bedclothing about which they need concern themselves is a sufficiency to cover them, forgetting that a man has an under as well as an upper side to keep warm, and must therefore have clothing between him and the earth, as well as between him and the air. Indeed, on trying the experiment, and rolling oneself up in a single blanket, the undermost side in a cold night is found to be by far the colder of the two. The substance of the blanket is compressed by the weight of the sleeper; the interstices between its fibers cease to exist, and the air which they contained and which is a powerful non-conductor of heat is squeezed out. Consequently wherever the blanket is compressed, its power of retaining the heat of the sleeper is diminished. Soft fleecy substances, like eiderdown quilts, which are extremely warm as coverlets, are well-nigh useless as mattresses.

There is another cause why a sleeper requires more protection from below than from above: it is that if the ground be at all wet, its damp will penetrate through very thick substances laid upon it. It will therefore be clearly understood that the object of a mattress is not alone to give softness to the bed, but also to give warmth; and that if a man lies in a hammock, with only the hammock below, and blankets above, he will be fully as much chilled as if the arrangement had been reversed, and he had lain upon blankets with only the hammock as a sheet to cover him.

☞ The oldest travelers are ever those who go the most systematically to work in making their sleeping places dry and warm. Unless a traveler makes himself at home and comfortable in the bush, he will never be quite contented with his lot, but will fall into the bad habit of looking forwards to the end of his journey, and to his return to civilization, instead of complacently interesting himself in its continuance. This is a frame of mind in which few great journeys have been successfully accomplished, and an explorer who cannot divest himself of it may suspect that he has mistaken his vocation.

☞ The vital heat of a man, either in an active or a latent form, is equal to that which is given out by two ordinary

☞ Straw, well knitted or plaited together, forms a good mattress, commonly called a palliasse.

☞ Eight pounds' weight of shavings make an excellent bed, and I find I can cut them with a common spokeshave, in 3½ hours, out of a log of deal. It is practicable to make an efficient spokeshave by tying a large clasp-knife on a common stick which has been cut into a proper shape to receive it.

MATTRESSES AND THEIR SUBSTITUTES.

A strip of macintosh. If a traveler can do so, he should make a point of having a strip of macintosh sheeting 7 feet by 4, certainly not less than 6 feet by 3, to lay on the ground below his bedding. Macintosh, of the sort that suits all climates, and made of linen, not of silk, is invaluable to an explorer, whether in the form of sheeting, coats, water bags, swimming belts, or inflatable boats. A little box full of the composition for mending it, and a spare bit of macintosh, should always be taken.

Mattress. Making a mattress is indeed a very simple affair. A bag of canvas, or other cloth, is made of the size wanted. It is then stuffed full of hair, wool, dry leaves, or cotton, and a strong stitch is put through it every few inches. The use of the stitching is to prevent the stuffing from being displaced and forming lumps in different parts of the bag.

Various makeshifts. If a traveler, as is very commonly the case, should have no mattress, he should strew his sleeping place with dry grass plucked up from the ground, or with other things warm to the touch, imitating the structure of a bird's nest as far as he has skill and materials to do so. Leaves, fern, feathers, heather, rushes, flags of reeds and of maize, wood shavings, bundles of faggots, and such like materials as chance may afford, should be looked for and appropriated; a pile of stones, or even two trunks of trees rolled close together, may make a dry bedstead in a marshy land. Over these, let him lay whatever empty bags, skins, saddlecloths, or spare clothes he may have, which from their shape or smallness cannot be turned to account as coverings, and the lower part of his bed is complete.

If a night of unusual cold be expected, the best use to make of spare wearing apparel is to put it on over that which is already on the person. With two or three shirts, stockings, and trousers, though severally of thin materials, a man may get through a night of very trying weather.

PREPARING THE GROUND FOR A BED.

Travelers should always root up the stones and sticks that might interfere with the smoothness of the place where they intend to sleep. This is a matter worth taking a great deal of pains about; the oldest campaigners are the most particular in making themselves comfortable at night. They should also scrape a hollow in the ground, of the shape shown in fig. 2, before spreading their sleeping rugs. It is disagreeable enough to lie on a perfectly level surface, like that of a floor, but the acme of discomfort is to lie upon a convexity. Persons who have omitted to make a shapely lair for themselves should at least scrape a hollow in the ground just where the hip bone would otherwise press.

COVERLETS.

General remarks. For an upper cover, it is of importance to an otherwise unsheltered person that its texture should be such as to prevent the wind blowing through. If it does so, no thickness is of any avail in keeping out the cold; hence the advantage of skin carosses, buffalo robes, leather sheets, and macintosh rugs. All cloths lose much of their closeness of texture in a hot, dry climate; the fibers

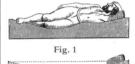

Fig. 1

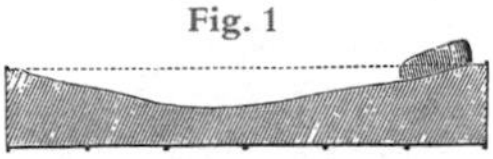

Fig. 2

☞ The annexed sketch *(fig. 1)* represents a man sleeping in a natural attitude. It will be observed that he fits into a concavity of about 6 inches in greatest depth. (The scale on which he is drawn is 6 feet long and 1 foot high.)

☞ It is in order to make their coverings windproof that shepherd lads on the hills in Scotland, when the nights are cold, dip their plaids in water before sitting or lying down in them. The wet swells up the fibers of the plaid and makes the texture of it perfectly dense and close.

☞ If a man be destitute of proper wraps, he cannot do better than put on all the spare clothes he possesses. The additional warmth of a single extra shirt is remarkable.

☞ However wet the weather may be during the day, the traveler should never relax his endeavors to keep a dry and warm change of clothes for his bivouac at night. Hardships in rude weather matter little to a healthy man, when he is awake and moving, and while the sun is above the horizon; but let him never forget the deplorable results that may follow a single night's exposure to cold, malaria, and damp.

shrink extremely, and the wind blows through the tissue as through network.

It is also of importance that the outer covering should have a certain weight, so as not to be too easily displaced, either by the person fidgeting in his sleep or by the blowing of the wind. In dry weather there is nothing like furs, but in a rainy country I prefer a thick blanket bag, a large spare blanket, and a macintosh sheet and counterpane. It may be objected that the bag and macintosh would be close and stuffy, but be assured that the difficulty when sleeping on mother earth, on a bitter night, is to keep the fresh air out, not to let it in. On fine nights I should sleep on the bag and under the spare blanket.

Stuffy bedding. It must be understood that while recommending coverlets that resist the wind, I am very far from advocating extreme stuffiness, and for the following reason. Though a free passage of the wind abstracts an excessive amount of animal heat from the sleeper, yet the freshness of pure air stimulates his body to give it out in an increased proportion. On the other hand, sleeping clothes that are absolutely impervious to the passage of the wind necessarily retain the cutaneous excretions: these poison the sleeper, acting upon his blood through his skin, and materially weaken his power of emitting vital heat; the fire of his life burns more languidly. There is, therefore, an intermediate arrangement of sleeping gear, neither too stuffy on the one hand nor too open on the other, by which the maximum power of resisting the chill of the night is obtainable.

Pillows. A mound of sand or earth, scraped together for a pillow, is ground down into flatness after a few minutes. A bag filled with earth, or it may be with grass, keeps its shape. Many people use their saddles as pillows; they roll up the flaps and stirrups and place the saddle on the ground with a stone underneath, at its hindmost end, to keep it level and steady, and then lay their heads on the seat. I prefer using anything else, as, for instance, the stone without the saddle, but I generally secure some bag or other for the purpose, as, without a pillow, it is difficult to sleep in comfort. A bag shaped like a pillowcase, and stuffed with spare clothes, is very convenient. Some people advocate aircushions.

SLEEPING BAGS.

Knapsack bags. These have been used for the last twenty-five years by the French douaniers who watch the mountain passes of the Pyrenean frontier. The bags are made of sheepskin with the wool inside. When not in use they are folded up and buckled with five buckles into the shape of a somewhat bulky knapsack, which the recent occupant may shoulder and walk away with.

Beds used to be almost unknown in some parts of the Pyrenees. Sheepskin sleeping bags were employed instead. Thus, I am assured that at the beginning of this century there was hardly a bed in the whole of the little republic of Andorre.

In fig. 1 the wide opening to the mouth of the bag is shown; also the ends of the buckles and straps that are sewn (on patches of leather, for additional strength) to the lower side of the bag, as seen in fig. 2. It must be understood that the woolly sides of the

☞ Brown paper is an excellent non-conductor of heat and excluder of drafts: English cottagers often enclose sheets of it within their quilted counterpanes. If thoroughly soaked and then dried, it will not crackle.

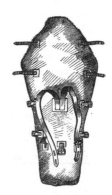

Fig. 1

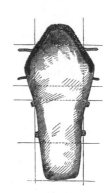

Fig. 2

Fig. 3

☞ I should think that a combination of a sleeping bag with a very small tent, just large enough to enclose the man's head and shoulders, so as to permit him to eat or write when lying in his bag without fear of the wet, would be the smallest and lightest arrangement compatible with efficiency in a stormy climate.

skins are inwards. The straps that hold the knapsack to the shoulders are secured by a simple fastening, shown in figs. 2 and 3. But the ordinary knapsack hooks and rings, if procurable, would answer the purpose better. The straight lines in fig. 1 show the way in which the bag is to be folded into the shape of fig. 3.

Macintosh sack. Mr. Falconer writes to me as follows:

> I traveled in 1841 from Austin in Texas to Mexico through New Mexico. I left Austin in June, and reached Zacatecas on Christmas Day. During nearly the whole period we traveled from Austin to New Mexico, I camped without any covering at night for myself, except a large macintosh, made up as a sack, with a piece so laid as a continuation of one side, as to be used as a coverlet, sufficient in length to be brought from the back, over the head, and down on the breast. Inside I placed my blankets. I slept under this covering during many a heavy storm at night, and got out of my soft-coated shell dry in the morning. My opinion is, that every traveler who works his way with a horse should fix on his own saddle the said macintosh sack, two blankets, a tin cup, and a frying-pan. It is amazing, when you get into real working order, how few things are sufficient.

Peasants' sack. The peasants in the northern parts of Germany use a strong linen sack made to draw at one end. This they stuff with straw, hay, dry leaves, &c., and, putting their feet into it, pull its mouth up to their armpits. They use them when driving their wagons in winter and when lodging at their wretched roadside inns.

BIVOUAC

Bivouacking is miserable work in a wet or unhealthy climate, but in a dry and healthy one there is no question of its superiority over tenting. Men who sleep habitually in the open breathe fresher air and are far more imbued with the spirit of wild life than those who pass the night within the stuffy enclosure of a tent. It is an endless pleasure to lie half awake watching the stars above and the picturesque groupings of the encampment round about, and to hear on all sides the stirrings of animal life. And later in the night, when the fire is low, and servants and cattle are asleep, and there is no sound but of the wind and an occasional plaintive cry of wild animals, the traveler finds himself in that close communion with nature which is the true charm of wild travel. Now all this pleasure is lost by sleeping in a tent. Tent life is semi-civilization, and perpetuates its habits. This may be illustrated by a simple trait; a man who has lived much in bivouacs, if there be a night alarm, runs naturally into the dark for safety, just as a wild animal would; but a man who travels with tents becomes frightened when away from its lights or from the fancied security of its walls.

SHELTER FROM THE WIND.

Study the form of a hare! In the flattest and most unpromising of fields, the creature will have availed herself of some little hollow to the lee of an insignificant tuft of grass, and there she will have nestled and fidgeted about till she has made a smooth, round, grassy bed, compact and fitted to her shape, where she may curl herself snugly up, and

SHELTER FROM THE WIND.

SHELTER FROM THE SKY.

VARIOUS METHODS OF BIVOUACKING.

IMPORTANCE OF COMFORT.

BIVOUAC IN SPECIAL LOCALITIES.

☞ In a dangerous country there can be no comparison between the hazard of a tent and that of a bivouac. In the former a man's sleep is heavy; he cannot hear nearly so well; he can see nothing; his cattle may all decamp; while marauders know exactly where he is lying, and may make their plans accordingly. They may creep up unobserved and spear him through the canvas.

☞ The first Napoleon had a great opinion of the advantages of bivouacking over those of tenting. He said it was the healthier of the two for soldiers.

☞ A common mistake of a novice lies in selecting a tree for his camping place, which spreads out nobly above, but affords no other shelter from the wind than that of its bare stem below. It may be that as he walks about in search of shelter, a mass of foliage at the level of his eye, with its broad shadow, attracts him, and as he stands to the leeward of it it seems snug, and, therefore, without further reflection, he orders his bed to be spread at the foot of some tree. But as soon as he lies down on the ground the tree proves worthless as a screen against the wind; it is a roof, but it is not a wall.

cower down below the level of the cutting night wind. Follow her example. A man, as he lies upon his mother earth, is an object so small and low that a screen of 18 inches high will guard him securely from the strength of a storm.

The real want in blowy weather is a dense low screen, perfectly wind-tight, as high as the knee above the ground. Thus, if a traveler has to encamp on a bare turf plain, he need only turn up a sod 7 feet long by 2 feet wide, and if he succeeds in propping it on its edge, it will form a sufficient shield against the wind.

Again, in selecting a place for bivouac, we must bear in mind that a gale never blows in level currents, but in all kinds of curls and eddies, as the driving of a dust storm, or the vagaries of bits of straw caught up by the wind, unmistakably show us. Little hillocks or undulations combined with the general lay of the ground are a chief cause of these eddies; they entirely divert the current of the wind from particular spots. Such spots should be looked for; they are discovered by watching the grass or the sand that lies on the ground. If the surface be quiet in one place, while all around it is agitated by the wind, we shall not be far wrong in selecting that place for our bed, however unprotected it may seem in other respects.

SHELTER FROM THE SKY.

The shelter of a wall is only sufficient against wind or driving rain; we require a roof to shield us against vertical rain and against dew, or what is much the same thing, against the cold of a clear blue sky on a still night. The temperature of the heavens is known pretty accurately by more than one method of calculation: it is -289° Fahr.; the greatest cold felt in the Arctic regions being about -40° Fahr. If the night be cloudy, each cloud is a roof to keep off the cold; if it be clear, we are exposed to the full chill of the blue sky with only such alleviation as the warming and the non-conducting powers of the atmosphere may afford.

The effect is greater than most people would credit. The uppermost layer of the earth, or whatever may be lying exposed upon it, is called upon to part with a great quantity of heat. If it so happen that the uppermost layer is of a non-conducting nature, the heat abstracted from it will be poorly resupplied by communication from the lower ones. Again, if the night be a very calm one, there will be no supply of warmth from fresh currents of air falling down upon it. Hence, in the treble event of a clear blue sky, a non-conducting soil, and a perfectly still night, we are liable to have great cold on the surface of the ground. This is shared by a thin layer of air that immediately rests upon it, while at each successive inch in height the air becomes more nearly of its proper temperature.

VARIOUS METHODS OF BIVOUACKING.

Unprotected. Mr. Shaw, the traveler in Tibet, says:

My companion and I walked on to keep ourselves warm, but halting at sunset, had to sit and freeze several hours before the things came up. The best way of keeping warm on such an occasion, is to squat down, kneeling against a bank, resting your head on the bank, and nearly between your knees. Then tuck your overcoat in, all round you, over head and all; and if you are lucky, and there is not too much wind, you will make a little atmosphere of your own inside the covering,

☞ It is constantly remarked that a very slight mound or ridge will shelter the ground for many feet behind it, and an old campaigner will accept such shelter gladly, notwithstanding the apparent insignificance of its cause.

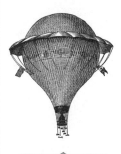

In this section of the original book, Galton refers to experiments on ground temperature and humidity made by meteorologist **James Glaisher** (British, 1809-1903). In 1845, Glaisher published the first dew point tables. He also measured temperature and humidity at elevation in a hot air balloon. In 1862 he ascended to an estimated seven miles above sea level, ostensibly breaking the world record for altitude, but passed out before taking a precise reading.

which will be snug in comparison with the outside air. Your feet suffer chiefly, but you learn to tie yourself into a kind of knot, bringing as many surfaces of your body together as possible. I have passed whole nights in this kneeling position, and slept well; whereas I should not have got a wink had I been stretched at full length with such a scanty covering as a great-coat.

Bushes. I have shown that the main object before sleeping out at night is to secure a long wind-tight wall, and that the next is to obtain a roof. Both these objects may be attained by pleaching two or three small neighboring bushes into one; or branches may be torn off elsewhere and interwoven between the bushes. A few leafy boughs, cut and stuck into the ground, with their tops leaning over the bed, and secured in that position by other boughs, wattled in horizontally, give great protection. Long grass, &c., should be plucked and strewn against them to make them as wind-tight as possible.

Walls. A pile of saddle bags and other traveling gear may be made into a good screen against the wind, and travelers usually arrange them with that intention. Walls of stone may be built as a support to cloths, whose office it is to render the walls wind-tight, and also by lapping over their top to form a partial roof. The Tibetan traveler cares for no roof overhead if he can shelter himself from the wind behind a three-foot wall. Hence the numerous little enclosures clustered together like cells of a honeycomb at every halting-place, with one side always raised

against the prevailing wind. (Shaw.) These walls are built round shallow pits, each with its rough fireplace in the middle.

Cloths. Any cloth may be made to give shelter by an arrangement like that in the sketch. The corners of the cloth should be secured by simple hitches in the rope, and never by knots. The former are sufficient for all purposes of security, but the latter will jam, and you may have to injure both cloth and string to get them loose again. It is convenient to pin the sides of the cloth with a skewer round the ropes. Any strip of wood makes a skewer. Earth should be banked against the lowest edge of the cloth to keep out the wind and to prevent its flapping. The sticks may, on an emergency, be replaced by faggots of brushwood, by guns, or by ropes carried down from the overhanging branches of a tree.

IMPORTANCE OF COMFORT.

To conclude these general hints, let the traveler, when out in trying weather, work hard at making his sleeping place perfectly dry and comfortable; he should not cease until he is convinced that it will withstand the chill of the early morning, when the heat of the yesterday's sun is exhausted, and that of the coming sun has not begun to be felt. It is wretched beyond expression for a man to lie shivering beneath a scanty covering and to feel the night air become hourly more raw, while his life-blood has less power to withstand it; and to think, self-reproachfully, how different would have been his situation if he had simply had forethought and energy enough to cut and draw twice the quantity

It is wretched beyond expression for a man to lie shivering beneath a scanty covering and to feel the night air become hourly more raw, while his life-blood has less power to withstand it

of firewood, and to spend an extra half-hour in laboring to make himself a snugger berth. The omission once made becomes irreparable; for in the cold of a pitiless night he has hardly sufficient stamina to rise and face the weather, and the darkness makes him unable to cope with his difficulties.

BIVOUAC IN SPECIAL LOCALITIES.

Encampment in forests. A clump of trees yields wonderful shelter. The Swedes have a proverb that "the forest is the poor man's jacket." In firwoods there is great facility in making warm encampments, for a young tree, when it is felled, yields both poles to support branches for shields against weather, and finer cuttings for flooring above the snow or damp. A common plan is to support a crossbar by two uprights, as shown in the figure; against this crossbar a number of poles are made to lean; on the back of the poles abundance of fir branches are laid horizontally; and lastly, on the back of these are another set of leaning poles, in order to secure them by their weight.

On bare plains. Avoid sleeping in slight hollows during clear still weather. The cold stratum of air pours down into them, like water from the surrounding plain, and stagnates. Spring frosts are always more severely felt in hollows. Therefore, in a broad level plain, especially if the night be clear and calm, look out for some slightly rising ground for an encampment. The chilled stratum of air drains from off it, and is replaced by warmer air. Horses and cattle, as the night sets in, always draw up to these higher grounds, which rise like islands through the sea of mist that covers the plain.

☞ Walls have been built for shelter against the wind, on a bare sandy plain, by taking empty bags, filling them with sand, and then building them up as if they had been stones.

Buried, or in holes. A European can live through a bitter night, on a perfectly dry sandy plain, without any clothes besides what he has on, if he buries his body pretty deeply in the sand, keeping only his head above ground. It is a usual habit of the naked natives in Australia to do so, and not an unfrequent one of the Hottentots of South Africa. Mr. Moffat◆ records with grateful surprise how he passed a night, of which he had gloomy forebodings, in real comfort, even luxury, by adopting this method. A man may be as comfortable in a burrow as in a den.

In arid countries, dry wells, dug by natives and partially choked by drifted sand, are often to be met with. They are generally found near existing watering places, where they have been superseded by others, better placed and deeper. Now, there are few warmer sleeping places than one of these dry wells; a small fire is easily kept burning at the bottom, and the top may be partially roofed over.

In ashes of campfire. A few chill hours may be got over, in a plain that affords no other shelter, by nestling among the ashes of a recently burnt-out camp fire.

By rocks. In the cruel climate of Tibet, Dr. Hooker◆ tells us that it is the habit to encamp close to some large rock, because a rock absorbs heat all day and parts with it but slowly during the nighttime. It is, therefore, a reservoir of warmth when the sun is down, and its neighborhood is coveted in the nighttime. Owing to the same cause, acting in the opposite direction, the shadow of a broad rock is peculiarly cool and grateful during the heat of the day in a thirsty land.

Galton may be referring to **Reverend Robert Moffat,** one of the first missionaries in Africa. He lived for fifty years in Kuruman, a town in South Africa's Kalahari Desert, and established a mission there. Moffatt's daughter, Mary, was married in its church to the missionary and explorer David Livingstone.

Sir Joseph Dalton Hooker (British, 1817-1911) completed medical training, but after joining an expedition to the Antarctic he devoted himself to botany. Hooker studied plant life on expeditions to India, Palestine, Morocco, and the U.S. and published many botanical reference books; he became a leader in the scientific community and was named director of the Royal Botanical Gardens at Kew and president of the Royal Society. Hooker was among those who urged Darwin to publish his work on evolution and natural selection, and gave public support to Darwin's

☞ In Napoleon's retreat, after his campaign in Russia, many a soldier saved or prolonged his life by creeping within the warm and reeking carcass of a horse that had died by the way.

On heather. Mr. St. John tells us of an excellent way in which Highland poachers, when in a party, usually pass frosty nights on the moorside. They cut quantities of heather, and strew part of it as a bed on the ground; then all the party lie down, side by side, excepting one man, whose place among the rest is kept vacant for him. His business is to spread plaids upon them as they lie, and to heap up the remainder of the heather upon the plaids. This being accomplished, the man wriggles and works himself into the gap that has been left for him in the midst of his comrades.

On snow. Dr. Kane says:

We afterwards learnt to modify and reduce our traveling-gear, and found that in direct proportion to its simplicity and to our apparent privation of articles of supposed necessity, were our actual comfort and practical efficiency. Step by step, as long as our Arctic service continued, we went on reducing our sledging outfit, until we at last came to the Eskimo ultimatum of simplicity—raw meat and a fur bag.

☞ It appears that people may bury themselves in snow, and want neither air nor warmth. I have never made the experiment, but have read of numerous instances of people falling into snowdrifts and not being extricated for many days, and when at length they were taken out, they never seem to have complained of cold or any other sufferings than those of hunger and of anxiety.

TENTS

Although tents are not worth the trouble of pitching on dry nights in a healthy climate, they are invaluable protectors to a well-equipped traveler against rain, dew, and malaria. But a man who is not so equipped, who has no change of clothes and no bedstead to sleep on, will do better to sleep in the open air in front of a good campfire. Napoleon I, speaking of soldiers, says:

> *Tents are not healthy; it is better for the soldier to bivouac, because he sleeps with his feet to the fire, whose neighborhood quickly dries the ground on which he lies; some planks or a little straw shelter him from the wind. Nevertheless a tent is necessary for superior officers; who have need to write and to consult a map. (Maximes de Guerre)*

It is very convenient that a tent should admit of being pitched in more than one form: for instance, that one side should open and form an awning in hot weather; also, that it should be easy to attach flys or awning to the tent to increase its available size during the daytime. All tents should be provided with strong covers, for pack ropes are sure to fray whatever they press against; and it is better that the cover should suffer than the tent itself.

COMPARATIVE SIZE OF TENTS.

The annexed diagram will show the points on which the roominess of a tent mainly depends. A man wants space to sit at a table, and also to get at his luggage in order either to pack it or to unpack it; lastly, he wants a reasonable amount of standing room. A fair-sized tent ought to include the figures drawn in the diagram, and I have indicated,

COMPARATIVE SIZE OF TENTS.

TENT VARIATIONS.

PITCHING A TENT.

PREPARATIONS FOR A STORM.

TO WARM TENTS.

PERMANENT CAMP.

LOST ARTICLES.

☞ To a party encamped for a few days, tents are of great use as storehouses for property, which otherwise becomes scattered about, at the risk of being lost or pilfered.

☞ When considering how much weight it will be possible to carry, it must be borne in mind that the tent will become far heavier than it is found to be in the peculiarly dry atmosphere of a tent-maker's showroom.

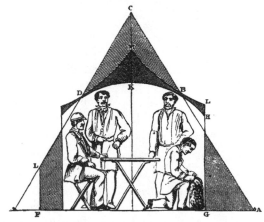

by lines and shaded spaces, the section of various descriptions of tents that would be just sufficient to embrace them.

Small tents. For tents of the smallest size and least pretensions, nothing can be better than the one represented in fig. 1: the ends are slit down their middles, and are laced or buttoned together, so that, by unfastening these, the tent spreads out to a flat sheet of the form of fig. 2, well adapted for an awning, or else it can be simply unrolled and used with the bedding. It is necessary that a tent should be roomy enough to admit of a man undressing himself, when wet through, without treading upon his bed and drenching it with mud and water; and therefore a tent of the above description is found to be unserviceable if less than 7 feet long, or ending in a triangle of less than 52 feet in the side.

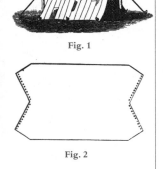

Fig. 1

Fig. 2

TENT VARIATIONS.

Pitched over an excavation. A hole may be dug deeply beneath the tent floor, partly for the pur–

pose of a storeroom, and partly for that of a living room when the weather is very inclement. This was practiced before Sebastopol in the manner shown in the figure. The notched pole acts as a ladder for ascending from below.

Gypsy tent. A traveler who has only a blanket, a plaid, or broad piece of material of any kind, with which he wishes to improvise a tent, may make a framework of long wands, planting their ends in the ground, bending their tops together, and lashing or wattling them securely; over this the blanket is thrown *(fig. 3)*. If the sticks are sufficiently long and pliant, their ends should be bent over the roof half-way down the opposite side, as in fig. 1. This adds considerably to the strength of the arrangement.

The gypsies in England use the following excellent contrivance to save the trouble of tying the sticks together. They carry a light bar of wood, 22 feet long, bound with string here and there to keep it from splitting; through this, six holes, each big enough to admit the tip of the little finger, are bored or burnt; they also carry eight hazel rods with them, each 6 feet long, and arrange their framework as in fig. 2. It will be observed that the two rods which are planted behind give additional roominess and stability to the affair. The rug and pillow show the position in which the occupants sleep. Blankets, not sheeting, pinned together with wooden pegs, are thrown over the whole, as in fig. 3.

Fig. 1

Fig. 2

Tent of mosquito netting. I have been informed of a sportsman in Ceylon who took with him into the woods a cot with mosquito curtains as a protection

Fig. 3

*A tent should
never be pitched
in a slovenly way*

☞ It is wonderful how men
will bungle with a tent when
they are not properly drilled
to pitch it.

☞ Tent pegs should be of
galvanized iron; they are well
worth the weight of carriage,
for not only do wooden ones
often fail on an emergency, but
cooks habitually purloin them
when firewood is scarce.

not only against insects, but against malaria. He also
had a blanket rolled at his feet; at three in the morning, when the chill arose in the woods, he pulled his
blanket over him.

PITCHING A TENT.

It is quite an art so to pitch a tent as to let in
or exclude the air, to take advantage of sun and
shade, &c. &c. Every available cloth or sheet may be
pressed into service to make awnings and screens.
There is a great deal of character shown in each
different person's encampment. A tent should never
be pitched in a slovenly way: it is so far more roomy,
secure, and pretty when tightly stretched out, that
no pains should be spared in drilling the men to do
it well. I like to use a piece of string, marked with
knots, by which I can measure the exact places in
which the tent pegs should be struck, for the eye is
a deceitful guide in estimating squareness.

To secure tent ropes. When the soil is loose,
scrape away the surface sand before driving the tent
pegs. Loose mold is made more tenacious by pouring water upon it. When one peg is insufficient, it
may be backed by another. *(See fig.)* The outermost
peg must be altogether buried in the earth. Heavy
saddlebags are often of use to secure the tent ropes
and, in rocky ground, heavy piles of stones may be
made to answer the same purpose. The tent ropes
may also be knotted to a cloth on which stones are
afterwards piled.

"Dáterám" is, as the late Dr. Barth informed
me, the Bornu name for a most excellent African
contrivance, used in some parts of the Sahara desert,

by means of which tent ropes may be secured, or horses picketed in sand of the driest description, as in that of a sand dune, whence a tent peg would be drawn out by a strain so slight as to be almost imperceptible. I have made many experiments upon it and find its efficiency to be truly wonderful. The plan is to tie to the end of the tent rope a small object of any description, by its middle, as a short stick, a stone, a bundle of twigs, or a bag of sand and to bury it from 1 to 2 feet in the loose sand. It will be found, if it has been buried 1 foot deep, that a strain equal to about 50 lbs. weight is necessary to draw it up; if 12 feet deep, that a much more considerable strain is necessary; and that if 2 feet deep, it is quite impossible for a single man to pull it up.

To prevent tent poles from slipping. When the tent is pitched in the ordinary way on a smooth rocky surface, there is considerable danger that the foot of the pole may slip whenever a gust of wind or other sudden impulse sways the tent. This danger is to be obviated on precisely the same principle as that by which builders secure their scaffolding poles upon the smooth footways of a street: they put the foot of each pole into a bucket filled with sand. As the base of the bucket is broad, the scaffolding is much less liable to slip than if the narrow bases of the poles had rested directly upon the pavement.

To tie things to tent poles. To hang clothes, or anything else, upon a smooth tent pole, see "clove hitch" *(p. 167)*. A strap with hooks attached to it, buckled round the pole, is very convenient. The method shown in the sketch suffices if the pole be

☞ A broken tent pole can be mended permanently by placing a splint of wood on either side of the fracture, and by whipping the whole together with soft cord or with the untwisted strand of a piece of rope.

notched, or jointed, or in any way slightly uneven. Bags, &c., are supposed to be hung upon the bit of wood that is secured to the free end. Convenient pegs, made of bits of wood roughly sharpened, may be driven into the tree, if any, when the encampment is made.

PREPARATIONS FOR A STORM.

Before a storm, dig a ditch as deep as you can round the outside of the tent to divert the coming sheet of surface water, and see that the ditch has a good outfall. The ditch will also drain the floor of the tent if the rain should soak in. Even a furrow scratched with a tent peg is better than no ditch at all. Fasten guy ropes to the spike of the tent pole, and be careful that the tent is not too much on the strain, else the further shrinking of the materials, under the influence of the wet, will certainly tear up the pegs. Earth, banked up round the bottom of the tent, will prevent gusts of wind from finding their way beneath. It is also a good plan to prepare a small hole near the foot of the tent pole, with a stone firmly rammed into the bottom, into which the tent pole may be shifted as soon as the strain of the tent, under the influence of the wet, becomes dangerous to its safety.

TO WARM TENTS.

When living in a tent in Otago (New Zealand) during a severe winter, we were perfectly numb with cold at nights, until we adopted the Maori plan, which is to dig a hole about a foot square in the clear, to cover the bottom with a stone or stones, and to fill it at night with red hot cinders from the camp fire, and lastly, to close the tent excepting a small opening near the top. The cinders are not nearly burnt out by morning. They diffused a pleasant warmth through the tent, and rendered us comfortable all night. There is no danger of suffocation, unless the tent be closed up very tight indeed. (W. M. Cooper.)

PERMANENT CAMP.

The accompanying sketch shows a tent pitched for a lengthened habitation. It has a deep drain, a seat and table dug out, and a fireplace.

LOST ARTICLES.

Small articles are constantly mislaid and trampled in the sand of the floor of the tent. In searching for them, the ground should be disturbed as little as possible. It is a usual plan to score its surface in parallel lines, with a thin wand. It would be well worthwhile to make a small light rake to use for this purpose.

☞ For want of a chair it is convenient to dig a hole or a trench in the ground, and to sit on one side of it with the feet resting on its bottom. The opposite side of the trench serves as a table on which things may be put within easy reach.

☞ The art of luxurious tenting is better understood in Persia than in any other country, even than in India.

☞ The luxuries and elegances practicable in tent life are only limited by the means of transport. Julius Caesar, who was a great campaigner, carried parquets of wooden mosaic for his floors! The articles that make the most show for their weight are handsome rugs, skins, and pillows; canteens of dinner and coffee services; and candles with screens of glass or other arrangements to prevent them from flickering.

OUTFIT OF MEDICINES.

PRECAUTIONS IN UNHEALTHY PLACES.

ILLNESS AND MISHAPS.

LITTER FOR THE WOUNDED.

BUSH REMEDIES

OUTFIT OF MEDICINES.

A traveler, unless he be a professed physician, has no object in taking a large assortment of drugs. He wants a few powders, ready prepared, which a physician who knows the diseases of the country in which he is about to travel will prescribe for him.

PRECAUTIONS IN UNHEALTHY PLACES.

There are certain precautions which should be borne in mind in unhealthy places, besides regularly taking small doses of quinine, such as never to encamp to the leeward of a marsh; to sleep close in between large fires, with a handkerchief gathered round your face (natural instinct will teach this); to avoid starting too early in the morning; and to beware of unnecessary hunger, hardship, and exposure. It is a widely corroborated fact that the banks of a river and adjacent plains are often less affected by malaria than the low hills that overlook them.

☞ The traveler who is sick, away from help, may console himself with the proverb that "though there is a great difference between a good physician and a bad one, there is very little between a good one and none at all."

ILLNESSES AND MISHAPS.

Fevers of all kinds, diarrhea, and rheumatism are the plagues that most afflict travelers; ophthalmia often threatens them. Change of air, from the flat country up into the hills as soon as the first violence of the illness is past, works wonders in hastening and perfecting a cure.

Diarrhea. With a bad diarrhea take nothing but broth, rice water, and it may be rice, in very small quantities at a meal until you are quite restored. The least piece of bread or meat causes an immediate relapse.

Toothache. Tough diet tries the teeth so severely that a man about to undergo it should pay a visit to a dentist before he leaves England. An unskilled traveler is very likely to make a bad job of a first attempt at tooth-drawing. By constantly pushing and pulling an aching tooth, it will in time loosen, and perhaps, after some weeks, come out.

Thirst. Pour water over the clothes of the patient and keep them constantly wet; restrain his drinking, after the first few minutes, as strictly as you can summon heart to do it. In less severe cases, drink water with a teaspoon; it will satisfy a parched palate as much as if you gulped it down in tumblerfuls, and will disorder the digestion very considerably less.

Hunger. Give two or three mouthfuls, every quarter of an hour, to a man reduced to the last extremity by hunger; strong broth is the best food for him.

Poisoning. The first thing is to give a powerful emetic, that whatever poison still remains unabsorbed in the stomach may be thrown up. If there be violent pains and gripings, or retchings, give plenty of water to make the vomitings more easy. Next, do your best to combat the symptoms that are caused by the poison which was absorbed before the emetic acted. Thus, if the man's feet are cold and numbed, put hot stones against them and wrap them up warmly. If he be drowsy, heavy, and stupid, give brandy and strong coffee and try to rouse him. There is nothing more to be done, save to avoid doing mischief.

☞ Vapor baths are used in many countries, and the following plan, used in Russia, is often the most convenient. Heat stones in the fire and put them on the ground in the middle of the cabin or tent; on these pour a little water and clouds of vapor are given off. In other parts of the world branches are spread on hot wood embers and the patient is placed upon these, wrapped in a large cloth; water is then sprinkled on the embers and the patient is soon covered with a cloud of vapor. The traveler who is chilled or overworked, and has a day of rest before him, would do well to practice this simple and

☞ Emetics: for want of proper physic, drink a charge of gunpowder in a tumblerful of warm water or soapsuds, and tickle the throat.

Robert Barclay-Allardice
(British, 1779-1854), known as
Captain Barclay and also The
Celebrated Pedestrian, was a
notable Scottish walker of the
early 19th century. In 1809, on
a bet, he succeeded in walking
a mile every hour for 1,000
consecutive hours. For this
remarkable feat he won 1,000
guineas.

☞ M. Hermann Schlagint-
weit, who has had a great deal
of mountain experience in the
Alps and in the Himalayas, up
to the height of 20,000 feet or
more, tells me that he found
the headache, &c., come on
when there was a breeze,
far more than at any other
time. His whole party would
awake at the same moment,
and begin to complain of the
symptoms, immediately on the
commencement of a breeze.

Blistered feet. To prevent the feet from blistering,
it is a good plan to soap the inside of the stocking
before setting out, making a thick lather all over
it. A raw egg broken into a boot, before putting it
on, greatly softens the leather: of course the boots
should be well greased when hard walking is antici-
pated. After some hours on the road, when the feet
are beginning to be chafed, take off the shoes and
change the stockings, putting what was the right
stocking on the left foot and the left stocking on
the right foot. Or, if one foot only hurts, take off the
boot and turn the stocking inside out. These were
the plans adopted by Captain Barclay.◇ This recipe
is an excellent one; pedestrians and teachers of gym-
nastics all endorse it. When a blister is formed,

> *rub the feet, on going to bed, with spirits mixed with tallow
> dropped from a candle into the palm of the hand; on the
> following morning no blister will exist. The spirits seem to
> possess the healing power, the tallow serving only to keep
> the skin soft and pliant. This is Captain Cochrane's advice,
> and the remedy was used by him in his pedestrian tour.
> (Murray's◇ Handbook of Switzerland.)*

Rarefied air, effects of. On high plateaus or
mountains newcomers must expect to suffer. The
symptoms are described by many South American
travelers; the attack of them is there, among other
names, called the puna. The disorder is sometimes
fatal to stout plethoric people; oddly enough, cats
are unable to endure it: at villages 13,000 feet above
the sea, Dr. Tschudi says that they cannot live. Numerous trials have been made with these unhappy
feline barometers, and the creatures have been found
to die in frightful convulsions. The symptoms of the
puna are giddiness, dimness of sight and hearing,

headache, fainting fits, blood from mouth, eyes, nose, lips, and a feeling like seasickness. Nothing but time cures it. It begins to be felt severely at from 12,000 to 13,000 feet above the sea. The symptoms of over-work are not wholly unlike those of the puna, and many young travelers who have felt the first have ascribed them to the second.

Snake bites. Tie a string tight above the part, suck the wound, and caustic it as soon as you can. Or, for want of caustic, explode gunpowder in the wound; or else do what Mr. Mansfield Parkyns well

suggests, i.e., cut away with a knife, and afterwards burn out with the end of your iron ramrod, heated as near a white heat as you can readily get it. The arteries lie deep, and as such flesh may, without much danger, be cut or burnt into, as much as the fingers can pinch up. The next step is to use the utmost energy, and even cruelty, to prevent the patient's giving way to that lethargy and drowsiness which is the usual effect of snake poison, and too often ends in death.

Scurvy has attacked travelers even in Australia, and I have myself felt symptoms of it in Africa when living wholly on meat. Any vegetable diet cures it: lime juice, treacle, raw potatoes, and acid fruits are especially efficacious. Dr. Kane insists on the value of entirely raw meat as a certain anti-scorbutic: this is generally used by the Eskimos.

Wasp and scorpion stings. The oil scraped out of a tobacco pipe is a good application; should the

John Murray III (British, 1808-1892), the third Murray to head up the family publishing house, initiated the world's first comprehensive travel guide-book series, *Handbooks for Travellers*. During the Victorian era, fast-growing interest in foreign exploration of all kinds ensured the success of the handbooks, which were full of detailed information from literary lights of the time.

☞ A correspondent writes to me, "I have often found a light cotton or linen bag a great safeguard against the attacks of fleas. I used to creep into it, draw the loop tight round my neck, and was thus able to set legions of them at defiance."

When a man breaks a bone, do not convert a simple injury into a severe one by carrying him carelessly

scorpion be large, his sting must be treated like a snake bite.

Broken bones. It is extremely improbable that a man should die, in consequence of a broken leg or arm, if the skin be uninjured; but if the broken end forces its way through the flesh, the injury is a very serious one. Abscesses form, the parts mortify, and the severest consequences often follow. Hence, when a man breaks a bone, do not convert a simple injury into a severe one by carrying him carelessly. If possible, move the encampment to the injured man and not vice versa.

> *When a man has broken his leg, lay him on the other side, put the broken limb exactly on the sound one, with a little straw between, and tie the two legs together with handkerchiefs. Thus the two legs will move as one, and the broken bone will not hurt the flesh so much, nor yet come through the skin.* (Mr. Druitt.)

Immersion. A half-drowned man must be put to bed in dry, heated clothes, hot stones, &c., placed against his feet, and his head must be raised moderately. Human warmth is excellent, such as that of two big men made to lie close up against him, one on each side. All rough treatment is not only ridiculous but full of harm; such as the fashion—which still exists in some places—of hanging up the body by the feet, that the swallowed water may drain out of the mouth.

LITTER FOR THE WOUNDED.

If a man be wounded or sick, and has to be carried upon the shoulders of others, make a litter for him in the Indian fashion; that is to say, cut two stout poles, each 8 feet long, to make its two sides, and three other crossbars of 22 feet each, to be lashed to them. Then supporting this ladder-shaped framework over the sick man as he lies in his blanket, knot the blanket up well to it, and so carry him off palanquin-fashion. One crossbar will be just behind his head, another in front of his feet; the middle one will cross his stomach and keep him from falling out; and there will remain two short handles for the carriers to lay hold of. The American Indians carry their wounded companions by this contrivance after a fight, and during a hurried re-treat, for wonderful distances. A kind of wagon-roof top can easily be made to it, with bent boughs and one spare blanket.

TO MEASURE DISTANCE
BY TIME.

RATE OF MOVEMENT.

TRIANGULATION BY MEASURE-
MENT OF CHORDS.

MEASUREMENT OF TIME.

MEASUREMENTS

TO MEASURE DISTANCE BY TIME.

The pace of a caravan across average country is 21 statute, or 2 geographical, miles per hour, as measured with compasses from point to point, and not following the sinuosities of each day's course; but in making this estimate, every minute lost in stoppages by the way is supposed to be subtracted from the whole time spent on the road. A careful traveler will be surprised at the accuracy of the geographical results, obtainable by noting the time he has employed in actual travel.

Experience shows that 10 English miles per day, measured along the road—or, what is much the same thing, 7 geographical miles, measured with a pair of compasses from point to point—is, taking one day with another, and including all stoppages of every kind, whatever be their cause, very fast traveling for a caravan. In estimating the probable duration of a journey in an unknown country, or in arranging an outfit for an exploring expedition, not more than half that speed should be reckoned upon. Indeed, it would be creditable to an explorer to have conducted the same caravan for a distance of 1,000 geographical miles, across a rude country, in six months.

RATE OF MOVEMENT.

A man or a horse walking at the rate of one mile per hour, takes ten paces in some ascertainable number of seconds, dependent upon the length of his step. If the length of his step be 30 inches, he

☞ These data on rates of travel apply to an exploration of considerable length, in which a traveler must feel his way, and where he must use great caution not to exhaust his cattle, lest some unexpected call for exertion should arise, which they might prove unequal to meet. Persons who have never traveled—and very many of those who have, from neglecting to analyze their own performances—entertain very erroneous views on these matters.

will occupy 17 seconds in making 10 paces. Conversely, if the same person counts his paces for 17 seconds, and finds that he has taken 10 in that time, he will know that he is walking at the rate of exactly 1 mile per hour. If he had taken 40 paces in the same period, he would know that his rate had been 4 miles per hour; if 35 paces, that it had been 3.5, or 32 miles per hour. Thus it will be easily intelligible, that if a man knows the number of seconds appropriate to the length of his pace, he can learn the rate at which he is walking by counting his paces during that number of seconds and by dividing by 10 the number of his paces so obtained.

☞ Actual measurement with the rudest makeshift is far preferable to an unassisted guess, especially to an unpracticed eye.

Convenient equivalents. The rate of 1 mile per hour is the equivalent to each of the rates in the following list:

YARDS.	FEET.	INCHES.	
29.333	88.000	1,056.0	in 1 minute.
0.488	1.466	17.6	in 1 second.

Natural units of length. A man should ascertain his height; height of his eye above ground; ditto, when kneeling; his fathom; his cubit; his average pace; the span, from ball of thumb to tip of one of his fingers; the length of the foot; the width of two, three, or four fingers; and the distance between his eyes. In all probability, some one of these is an even and a useful number of feet or inches, which he will always be able to recollect and refer to as a unit of measurement.

☞ A stone's throw is a good standard of reference for greater distances.

☞ Cricketers estimate distance by the length between wickets.

☞ Pacing yards should be practiced.

The distance between the eyes is instantly determined and, I believe, never varies, while measurements of stature, and certainly those of girth of limb,

☞ It is well to dot or burn with the lens of your opera-glass a scale of inches on the gunstock and pocket knife.

The distance between the eyes is instantly determined, and, I believe, never varies

become very different when a man is exhausted by long travel and bad diet. It is therefore particularly useful for measuring small objects. To find it, hold a stick at arm's length, at right angles to the line of sight; then, looking past its end to a distant object, shut first one eye and then the other, until you have satisfied yourself of the exact point on the stick that covers the distant object as seen by the one eye, when the end of the stick exactly covers the same object, as seen by the other eye.

Velocity of sound. Sound flies at 380 yards or about 1,000 feet in a second, speaking in round numbers. It is easy to measure rough distances by the flash of a gun and its report, for even a storm of wind only makes four percent difference, one way or the other, in the velocity of sound.

TRIANGULATION BY MEASUREMENT OF CHORDS.

Colonel Everest, ◈ the late surveyor general of India, pointed out the advantage to travelers, unprovided with angular instruments, of measuring the chords of the angles they wish to determine. He showed that a person who desired to make a rude measurement of the angle C A B in the figure has

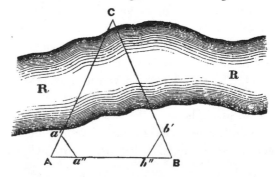

simply to pace for any convenient length from A towards C, reaching, we will say, the point a', and then to pace an equal distance from A towards B, reaching the point a'. Then it remains for him to pace the distance $a'a''$ which is the chord of the angle A to the radius A a'. Knowing this, he can ascertain the value of the angle C A B by reference to a proper table. In the same way the angle C B A can be ascertained. Lastly, by pacing the distance A B, to serve as a base, all the necessary data will have been obtained for determining the lines A C and B C. The problem can be worked out, either by calculation or by protraction. I have made numerous measurements in this way, and find the practical error to be within five percent.

MEASUREMENT OF TIME.

Sun dial. Plant a stake firmly in the ground in a level open space, and get ready a piece of string, a tent peg, and a bit of stick a foot long. When the stars begin to appear, and before it is dark, go to the stake, lie down on the ground, and plant the stick, so adjusting it that its top and the point where the string is tied to the stake shall be in a line with the Polar Star, or rather with the Pole *(see below)*; then get up, stretch the string so as just to touch the top of the stick, and stake it down with the tent peg. Kneel down again to see that all is right, and in the morning draw out the dial lines, the string being the gnomon. The true North Pole is distant about 1½ degree, or three suns' (or moons') diameters from the Polar Star, and it lies between the Polar Star and the pointers of the Great Bear, or, more truly, between it and Ursa Major.

Colonel Sir George Everest (Welsh, 1790-1866) was a geographer and surveyor who spent twenty-five years of his life on "The Great Survey": an exquisitely accurate mathematical description of the meridianal arc of India, extending some 1,500 miles from southern India to the Himalayas, at that time the longest survey project ever accomplished. The man who succeeded him as surveyor general in India used Everest's triangulation framework to pinpoint the summit of the world's highest peak, and in tribute to his predecessor's achievements named it Mount Everest. (Whether Everest ever saw the summit that bears his name is unknown.)

The one essential point of dial making is to set the gnomon truly, because it ensures that the shadows shall fall in the same direction at the same hours all the year round. To ascertain where to mark the hour lines on the ground, or wall, on which the shadow of the gnomon falls, the simplest plan is to use a watch or whatever makeshift means of reckoning time be at hand. Calculations are troublesome unless the plate is quite level, or vertical, and exactly facing south or north, or else in the plane of the Equinox.

The figure represents the well-known equinoctial sun dial. It can easily be cast in lead. The spike points towards the elevated pole, and the rim of the disc is divided into twenty-four equal parts for the hours.

WAYFINDING

BEARINGS BY COMPASS.

Pocket compass. One from 12 to 2 inches in diameter is practically the best. It should have plenty of depth, so that the card may traverse freely, even when the instrument is inclined; it should be light in weight, that it may not be easily jarred by a blow; and the catch that relieves the card, when the instrument is closed, should be self-acting and should act well. Lastly the movements of the needle should be quick; one that makes slow oscillations should be peremptorily refused, whatever its other merits may be. The graduation of the degrees on the card should be from 0° to 360°, north being 0° and east 90°.

Compass for use at night. The great majority of compasses are well-nigh useless in the dark, when it is most important to be able to consult them. They are rarely so constructed that the difference between the north and south sides is visible by moonlight or by the light of a cigar or piece of tinder. The more modern contrivances are very effective; in these the southern half of the compass card is painted black, the northern being left white. With a very faint light this difference can be appreciated.

BEARINGS BY SUN AND STARS.

It requires very great practice to steer well by stars, for, on an average, they change their bearings even faster than they change their altitudes. In tropical countries, the zodiacal stars, as Orion and Antares, give excellent east and west points. The

BEARINGS BY COMPASS.

BEARINGS BY SUN AND STARS.

OTHER SIGNS OF DIRECTION.

WAYSIDE MARKS ON TREES.

WAYSIDE MARKS WITH STONES.

GYPSY MARKS.

PAINT.

RECOLLECTION OF A PATH.

TO WALK IN A STRAIGHT LINE THROUGH FORESTS.

TO FIND THE WAY DOWN A HILLSIDE.

MIRAGE.

LOST PATH.

THEORY OF PATHFINDING.

☞ It is extraordinary how much the power of seeing a compass or a watch at night is increased by looking nearly at it through a magnifying glass.

☞ Errors in magnetic bearings: the compass needle is often found to be disturbed, and sometimes apparently bewitched, when laid upon hilltops, even when they consist of bare masses of granite. The disturbance is easily accounted for by the hornblende in the granite, or by other iron-bearing rocks. Explorers naturally select hills as their points of triangulation, but compass observations on hilltops, if unchecked by a sextant observation of the sun's bearings, are never so reliable as those taken on a plain.

☞ Moss grows best where there is continuous damp, therefore it prefers that side of a tree which affords the most suitable combination of exposure to damp winds and shelter from the sun. When the winds do not differ materially in dampness, the north side of the forest trees are the most thickly covered with moss.

Great Bear is useful when the North Pole cannot be seen, for you may calculate by the eye whereabout it would be in the heavens when its "pointers" were vertical, or due north; and the Southern Cross is available in precisely the same way. The true North Pole is about 12° or three diameters of the full moon apart from the Pole Star, and its place is on a line between the Pole Star and the Great Bear.

An almanac calculated to show the bearing, and the times of moonrise and moonset, for the country to be traveled over, as well as those of sunrise and sunset, would be a very great convenience; it would be worthwhile for a traveler accustomed to such calculations to make one for himself.

OTHER SIGNS OF DIRECTION.

Bearings by the growth of trees. In exposed situations and near the sea, the growth of trees is rarely symmetrical; they betray by their bent heads and stunted branches the direction of the prevalent influences most adverse to their growth. This direction is constant over wide districts in a flat country, but cannot be equally relied upon in a hilly one, where the mountains and valleys affect the conditions of shade and shelter and deflect the course of the wind.

Bearings by the shape of anthills. That most accurate observer, Pierre Huber,◈ writes as follows concerning the nests of the yellow ants, which are abundantly to be found in the Swiss Alps and in some other mountainous countries. It must be recollected, in reading his statement, that the chief occupation of ants is to move their eggs and larvae from one part of the nest to another to ensure them a warm and equable temperature; therefore, it is reasonable to expect that the nests of ants should be built on a uniform principle as regards their shape and aspect. Huber says:

> They serve as a compass to mountaineers when they are surrounded by thick mists, or have lost their way during the night; they do so in the following manner: The anthills (of the yellow ants), which are by far more numerous and more high in the mountains than anywhere else, are longer than they are broad, and are of a similar pattern in other respects. Their direction is invariably from east to west. Their highest point and their steepest side are turned towards the point of sunrise in the wintertime (au levant d'hiver), and they descend with a gradual slope in the opposite direction. I have verified these experiences of the shepherds upon thousands of anthills, and have found a very small number of exceptions; these occurred only in the case where the anthills had been disturbed by men or animals. The anthills do not maintain the constancy of their form in the lowlands, where they are more exposed to such accidents.

Ripple marks on snow or sand. The Siberians travel guided by the ripples in the snow, which run in a pretty fixed direction owing to the prevalence of a particular wind. The ripples in a desert of sand are equally good as guides; or the wind itself, if it happens to be blowing, especially to a person pushing through a tangled belt of forest. Before leaving a well-known track, and striking out at night into the broad open plain, notice well which way the wind blows as regards the course you are about to pursue.

Flight of birds. I have read somewhere that in the old days coasting sailors occasionally took pigeons with them, and when they had lost their bearings they let one fly, which it did at once to the land.

Jean Pierre Huber (Swiss, 1777-1840), an entomologist specializing in the study of ants, was the author of a seminal work, *Recherches sur les Moeurs des Fourmis Indigénes* (1810). He was the first to report on slavery in ant society.

☞ To follow a track at night: where the track is well marked, showers of sparks, ably struck with a flint and steel, are sufficient to show it, without taking the pains of making a flame.

☞ Smell of an old track: the earth of an old and well trodden road has a perceptible smell from the dung and trampling of animals passing over it, especially near to encampments. It is usual at night, when a guide doubts whether or no he is in the track, to take up handfuls of dirt and smell it. It is notorious that cattle can smell out a road.

WAYSIDE MARKS ON TREES.

Cutting marks. A very excellent "treeline" is made by cutting deep notches in a line of trees, starting from some conspicuous object, so that the notches will face the men that are to be guided by it; the trees must be so selected that three, or at least two of them, are in sight at once. The notch or sliced bark of a tree is called a "blaze" in bush language. These blazed trees are of much use as fingerposts on a dark night. They are best made by two persons, one chipping the trees on his right and the other those on his left. If the axes are quite sharp, they only need to be dropped against the tree in order to make the chip. Doing so hardly retards a person in his walking.

Another way more suitable to some kinds of forests is to strike the knife into the left side of the tree, to tear down a foot of bark, and to leave the bark hanging, for a double extent of white surface is shown in this way. Also, to break down tops of saplings and leave them hanging, the undersides of the leaves being paler than the upper, and the different lines of the reversed foliage make a broken bush to look unnatural among healthy trees, and it quickly arrests the attention.

Stamping marks. The keepers of some of the communal forests in Switzerland are provided with small axes, having the back of the axehead worked into a large and sharp die, the impression of the die being some letter or cipher indicating the commune. When these foresters wish to mark a tree, they give it first a slice with the edge of the axe, and then (turning the axe) they deal it a heavy blow

☞ A bundle of grass or twigs about 2 feet long, slung by its middle athwart a small tree at the level of the eye, by the side of a path, is well calculated to catch the attention. Its lines are so different to those seen elsewhere in the forest that it would be scarcely possible to overlook it.

☞ Boat or canoe trails: routes through lakes well studded with islands can be well marked by trimming conspicuous trees until only a tuft of branches is left at the top. This is called, in the parlance of the Far West, a "lopstick."

with the back of the axehead. By the first operation they prepare a clean surface for their mark, and by the second they stamp their cipher deeply into the wood.

Branding trees. Some explorers take branding irons and use them to mark each of their camping places with its number. This is especially useful in Australian travel, where the country is monotonous and there are few natives to tell the names of places.

WAYSIDE MARKS WITH STONES.

Marks cut on stone. I have observed a very simple and conspicuous permanent mark used in forest roads, as represented in the fig. The stone is 8 inches above ground, 32 wide, 8 long; the mark is black

and deeply cut. An arrowhead may be chiseled in the face of a rock and filled with melted lead. With a small "cold" chisel, 3 inches long and ¼ inch wide, a great deal of stone carving may readily be effected.

Piles of stones. Piles of stones are used by the Arabs in their deserts, and in most mountain tracts.

An immense length of the road, both in the government of the Don Cossacks and in that of Tambov, is marked out on a gigantic scale by heaps of stones, varying from 4 to 6 feet high. These are visible from a great distance; and it is very striking to see the

double row of them indicating the line of route over the Great Steppe—undulations which often

☞ Wooden crosses: a simple structure is put together with a single nail or any kind of lashing. It catches the attention immediately.

present no other trace of the hand of man. (Spottiswoode. ◈)

GYPSY MARKS.

When gypsies travel, the party that goes in advance leaves marks at crossroads in order to guide those who follow. These marks are called "patterans"; there are three patterans in common use. One is to pluck three large handfuls of grass and to throw them on the ground, at a short distance from one another, in the direction taken; another is to draw a cross on the ground, with one arm much longer than the rest, as a pointer—a cross is better than any other simple mark, for it catches many different lights. (In marking a road, do not be content with marking the dust—an hour's breeze or a shower will efface it—but take a tent peg, or sharpened stick, and fairly break into the surface, and your mark will be surprisingly durable.) The third of the gypsy patterans is of especial use in the dark: a cleft stick is planted by the roadside, close to the hedge, and in the cleft is an arm like a signpost. The gypsies feel for this at crossroads, searching for it on the lefthand side. (Borrow's◈ *Zincali.*) A twig, stripped bare, with the exception of two or three leaves at its end, is sometimes laid on the road with its bared end pointing forwards.

PAINT.

Whitewash, when mixed with salt, or grease, or glue size, will stand the weather for a year or more. It can be painted on a tree or rock; the rougher the surface on which it is painted, the longer will some sign of it remain.

William Spottiswoode (British, 1825-1883) was an eminent mathematician and sometime traveler. He was the author of *A Tarantasse Journey through Eastern Russia in the Autumn of 1856.* Spottiswoode followed Sir Joseph Hooker as president of the Royal Society (1878-1883).

George Henry Borrow (British, 1803-1881), a natural linguist, traveled throughout Europe all his life, studying languages and literature and writing accounts of his journeys, sometimes as fictional works. He was always absorbed by Romany culture: "I can remember no period when the mere mention of the name of Gypsy did not awaken within me feelings hard to be described," he wrote. "I cannot account for this—I merely state a fact." Borrow compiled a Romany dictionary and wrote *The Zincali: Or an Account of the Gypsies of Spain* (1841).

Black for inscriptions is made by mixing lamp-black with some kind of size, grease, wax, or tar. Dr. Kane, having no other material at hand, once burnt a large **K** with gunpowder on the side of a rock. It proved to be a durable and efficient mark. When letters are chiseled in a rock, they should be filled with black to make them more conspicuous.

Blood leaves a mark of a dingy hue that remains long upon a light-colored, absorbent surface, as upon the face of sandy rocks.

RECOLLECTION OF A PATH.

It is difficult to estimate by recollection only the true distances between different points in a road that has been once traveled over. There are many circumstances which may mislead, such as the accidental tedium of one part, or the pleasure of another; but besides these, there is always the fact that, in a long day's journey, a man's faculties of observation are more fresh and active on starting than later in the day when, from the effect of weariness, even peculiar objects will fail to arrest his attention. Now, as a man's recollection of an interval of time is, as we all know, mainly derived from the number of impressions that his memory has received while it was passing, it follows that, so far as this cause alone is concerned, the earlier part of his day's journey will always seem to have been disproportionately long compared to the latter.

TO WALK IN A STRAIGHT LINE THROUGH FORESTS.

Every man who has had frequent occasion to find his way from one place to another in a forest

☞ It is remarkable, on taking a long half-day's walk, and subsequently returning, after resting some hours, how long a time the earlier part of the return journey seems to occupy, and how rapidly different well-remembered points seem to succeed each other as the traveler draws homewards. In this case, the same cause acts in opposite directions in the two journeys.

William Wentworth Fitzwilliam, a.k.a. Viscount Milton,
(British, 1839-1877) and his
friend, Dr. Walter Cheadle,
co-authored *The North-West
Passage by Land: Being the
Narrative of an Expedition
from the Atlantic to the Pacific,
Undertaken with the View of
Exploring a Route Across the
Continent to British Columbia
through British Territory, by
One of the Northern Passes in
the Rocky Mountains.* Fitzwilliam was twenty-three and
Cheadle twenty-seven when
they undertook this year-long
journey; their account is
entertaining and was quite
popular. After their adventure,
Fitzwilliam became one of
the youngest members of the
House of Commons.

☞ The art of walking in a
straight line is possessed in
an eminent degree by good
plowmen. They always look
ahead and let the plow take
care of itself.

can do so without straining his attention. Thus, in
the account of Lord Milton's◈ travels, we read of
some North American Indians who were incapable
of understanding the white man's difficulty in keeping a straight line; but no man who has not had
practice can walk through trees in a straight line,
even with the utmost circumspection.

After making several experiments, I think the
explanation of the difficulty and the way of over-
coming it are as follows: if a man walks on a level
surface, guided by a single conspicuous mark, he is
almost sure not to travel toward it in a straight line;
his muscular sense is not delicate enough to guard
him from making small deviations. If, therefore,
after walking some hundred yards towards a single
mark, on ground that preserves his track, the traveler
should turn round, he will probably be astonished
to see how sinuous his course has been. However, if
he take note of a second mark and endeavor to keep
it strictly in a line with the first, he will easily keep
a perfectly straight course. But if he cannot find a
second mark, it will not be difficult for him to use
the tufts of grass, the stones, or the other accidents
of the soil in its place; they need not be precisely in
the same line with the mark, but some may be on
the right and some on the left of it, in which case, as
he walks on, the perspective of their change of position will be symmetrical.

Lastly, if he has not even one definite mark, but
is walking among a throng of forest trees, he may
learn to depend wholly on the symmetry of the
changes of perspective of the trees as a guide to his
path. He will keep his point of sight unchanged and

will walk in its direction, and if he deviates from that direction, the want of symmetry in the change of perspective on either side of the point on which he wishes to walk will warn him of his error. The appreciation of this optical effect grows easily into a habit. When the more distant view happens to be shut out, the traveler must regain his line under guidance similar to that by which a sailor steers who only looks at his compass at intervals—I mean by the aspect of the sky, the direction of the wind, and the appearance of the forest, when it has any peculiarity of growth dependent on direction. The chance of his judgment being erroneous to a small extent is the same on the right hand as on the left, consequently his errors tend to compensate each other.

TO FIND THE WAY DOWN A HILLSIDE.

If on arriving at the steep edge of a ridge, you have to take the caravan down into the plain, and it appears that a difficulty may arise in finding a good way for it, descend first yourself, as well as you can, and seek for a road as you climb back again. It is far more easy to succeed in doing this as you ascend than as you descend, because when at the bottom of a hill its bold bluffs and precipices face you, and you can at once see and avoid them, whereas at the top, these are precisely the parts that you overlook and cannot see.

MIRAGE.

When it is excessive, it is most bewildering: a man will often mistake a tuft of grass, or a tree, or other most dissimilar object for his companion, or

☞ Faintly marked paths over grass (blind paths) are best seen from a distance.

☞ Napoleon, when riding with his staff across a shallow arm of the Gulf of Suez, was caught in a fog; he utterly lost his way and found himself in danger. He thereupon ordered his staff to ride from him in radiating lines in all directions, and that such of them as should find the water to become more shallow should shout out.

As an assistant surgeon in the U.S. Navy, **Dr. Elisha Kent Kane** (American, 1820-1857) sailed to China, India, Africa, and South America, and served in the Mexican-American War—all before the age of thirty. From 1850-55 he joined two Arctic expeditions, the first as senior medical officer and the second as commander, in search of Sir John Franklin's lost party. Though unsuccessful in the rescue mission, Kane reached farther north than any party before him and contributed much valuable geographic information to those who pressed on to the North Pole. His two-volume *Arctic Explorations* was a huge bestseller, selling 20,000 copies in advance of publication.

his horse, or game. An old traveler is rarely deceived by mirage. If he doubts, he can in many cases adopt the following hint given by Dr. Kane◈: refraction will baffle a novice on the ice, but we have learned to baffle refraction. By sighting the suspected object with your rifle at rest, you soon detect motion.

LOST PATH.

If you fairly lose your way in the dark, do not go on blundering hither and thither till you are exhausted, but make as comfortable bivouac as you can and start at daybreak fresh on your search.

The bank of a watercourse, which is the best of clues, affords the worst of paths and is quite unfit to be followed at night. The ground is always more broken in the neighborhood of a river than far away from it, and the vegetation is more tangled. Explorers travel most easily by keeping far away from the banks of streams because then they have fewer broad tributaries and deep ravines to cross.

If in the daytime you find that you have quite lost your way, set systematically to work to find it. At all events, do not make the matter doubly perplexing by wandering further. Mark the place very distinctly where you discover yourself at fault, that it may be the center of your search. Be careful to ride in such places as will preserve your tracks. Break twigs if you are lost in a woodland; if in the open country, drag a stick to make a clear trail. Marks scratched on the ground to tell the hour and day that you passed by will guide a relieving party. A great smoke is useful for the same purpose and is visible for a long distance.

When the lost traveler is dead beat with fatigue, let him exert a strong control over himself, for if he gives way to terror, and wanders wildly about hither and thither, he will do no good and exhaust his vital powers much sooner. He should erect some signal, as conspicuous a one as he can with something fluttering upon it, sit down in the shade, and, listening keenly for any sound of succor, bear his fate like a man. His ultimate safety is merely a question of time, for he is sure to be searched for, and if he can keep alive for two or three days he will, in all probability, be found and saved.

☞ A man who loses himself, especially in a desert, is sadly apt to find his presence of mind forsake him, the sense of desolation is so strange and overpowering; but he may console himself with the statistics of his chance of safety–viz., that travelers, though constantly losing their party, have hardly ever been known to perish unrelieved.

THEORY OF PATHFINDING.

When you discover you are lost, ask yourself the following three questions: they comprise the *A B C* of the art of pathfinding, and I will therefore distinguish them by the letters *A*, *B*, and *C* respectively:

A. What is the least distance that I can with certainty specify within which the caravan-path, the river, or the seashore that I wish to regain lies?

B. What is the direction, in a vague general way, towards which the path or river runs or the sea coast tends?

C. When I last left the path, did I turn to the left or to the right?

As regards *A,* calculate coolly how long you have been riding or walking, and at what pace, since you left your party; subtract for stoppages and well-recollected zigzags; allow a mile and a half per hour for the pace when you have been loitering on foot,

When the lost traveler is dead beat with fatigue, let him exert a strong control over himself, for if he gives way to terror, he will do no good and exhaust his vital powers much sooner

and three and a half when you have been walking fast. Bear in mind that occasional running makes an almost inappreciable difference, and that a man is always much nearer to the lost path than he is inclined to fear.

A man is always much nearer to the lost path than he is inclined to fear

As regards *B,* if the man knows the course of the path to within eight points of the compass (or one fourth of the whole horizon), it is a great gain; or even if he knows *B* to within twelve points, say 120°, or one third of the whole horizon, his knowledge is available. For instance, let us suppose a man's general idea of the run of the path to be that it goes in a northerly and southerly direction; then if he is also positive that the path does not deviate more than to the N.E. on the one side of that direction, or to the N.W. on the other, he knows the direction to within eight points. Similarly, he is sure to twelve points, if his limits, on either hand, are E.N.E. and W.N.W. respectively.

C requires no further explanation.

Now, if a man can answer all three questions— *A, B* to within eight points of the compass, and *C*—he is four and a half times as well off as if he could only answer *A*. A knowledge of *B* in addition to *A* is of only one third the use that it would be if *C* also were known. The traveler who can only answer the questions *A* and *B,* but not *C,* must be prepared to travel from P to L and back again through P to M, a distance equal to 3 P L. If, however, he can answer the question *C,* he knows at once whether to travel towards L or towards M, and he has no return journey to fear. At the worst, he has simply to travel the distance P L.

The epitome of the whole is this: if you can only answer the question *A,* you must seek for the lost path by the tedious circle plan; or, what is the same, and a more manageable way of setting to work,

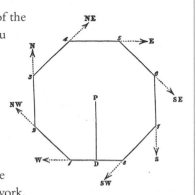

by traveling in an octagon, each side of which must be equal to four-fifths of P D. *(See fig.)* That is to say, look at your compass and start in any direction you please; we will say to the south, as represented in the drawing. Travel for a distance, P D; then, supposing you have not crossed the path, turn at right angles, and start afresh—we will suppose your present direction to be west—and travel for a distance four-tenths of P D, which will take you to *1;* then turn to the N.W. and travel for a distance eighttenths of P D, which will take you to *2;* then to the N. for a similar distance, which will take you to *3;* and so on, till the octagon has been completed. If you know *B* to eight points, and not *C,* adopt the L M system; also, if you know *A* and *C,* and *B* to within thirteen points (out of the sixteen that form the semicircle), you may still adopt the L M system; but not otherwise. A rough diagram scratched on the ground with a stick would suffice to recall the above remarks to a traveler's recollection.

REFLECTING THE SUN WITH A MIRROR.

FIRE SIGNALS.

OTHER SIGNALS.

SIGNALS

REFLECTING THE SUN WITH A MIRROR.

To attract the notice of a division of your party, five or even 10 miles off, glitter a bit of looking-glass in the sun, throwing its flash towards where you expect them to be. It is quite astonishing at how great a distance the gleam of the glass will catch the sharp eyes of a bushman who has learnt to know what it is. It is now a common signal in the North American prairies. (Sullivan.)

The signaler has to cause the disc of light to cover the person whose notice he wishes to attract. I will proceed to show how he can do so, but in the meantime it will be evident that a pretty careful aim is requisite, or he will fail in his object. It should be recollected that a passing flash has far less brilliancy than one that dwells for an appreciable time on the retina of the observer; therefore the signaler should do all he can to steady his aim. I find the steadiest way of holding the mirror is to rest the hand firmly against the forehead and to keep the eyes continually fixed upon the same distant object. When a flash is sent to a distant place, the size of the mirror is of no appreciable importance in affecting the size of the area over which the flash is visible.

To direct the flash of the mirror. There are makeshift ways of directing the flash of the mirror, as, by observing its play on an object some paces off, nearly in a line with the station it is wished to communicate with. In doing this, two cautions are requisite: first, the distance of the object must be so large compared to the diameter of the mirror

☞ The power of sun signals is extraordinarily great. A plane mirror only 3 inches across reflects as much of the sun as a globe of 120 feet diameter; it looks like a dazzling star at ten miles' distance.

☞ An object, in reality of a white color but apparently dark owing to its being shaded, shows the play of a mirror's flash better than any other.

that the play of the flash shall appear truly circular and exactly like a faint sun; secondly, be careful to bring the eye to the very edge of the mirror; there should be as little "dispart" as possible, as artillery-men would say. Unless these cautions be attended to very strictly, the flash will never be seen at the distant station.

Two bits of paper and a couple of sticks, arranged as in the drawing, serve pretty well to direct a flash. Sight the distant object through the holes in the two bits of paper, A and B, at the ends of the horizontal stick, and when you are satisfied that the stick is properly adjusted and quite steady, take your mirror and throw the shadow of A upon B, and further endeavor to throw the white speck in the shadow of A, corresponding to its pinhole in it, through the center of the hole in B. Every now and then lay the mirror aside and bend down to see that A B continues to be properly adjusted.

FIRE SIGNALS.

Fire beacons, hanging up a lantern, or setting fire to an old nest high up in a tree serve as night signals, but they are never to be depended on without previous concert, as bushes and undulations of the ground will often hide them entirely. The sparks from a well-struck flint and steel can be seen for much more than a mile.

The united holloa *of many voices, is heard much further than separate cries*

Smoke signals. The smoke of fires is seen very far by day; and green wood and rotten wood make the most smoke. It is best to make two fires 100 yards apart, lest your signaling should be mistaken for an ordinary fire in the bush. These double fires are a very common signal to vessels in the offing, on the African coast.

OTHER SIGNALS.

By sight. A common signal for a distant scout is that he should ride or walk round and round in a circle from right to left, or else in one from left to right.

Mr. Parkyns, ◈ speaking of Abyssinia, describes the habits of a caste of robbers in the following words:

> *At other times they will lie concealed near a road, with scouts in every direction on the lookout; yet no one venturing to speak, but only making known by signs what he may have to communicate to his companions or leader. Thus he will point to his ear and foot on hearing footsteps, to his eyes on seeing persons approach, or to his tongue if voices be audible; and will also indicate on his fingers the numbers of those coming, describing also many particulars as to how many porters, beasts of burden or for riding, there may be with the party.*

A kite has been suggested as a day signal; and also a kite with some kind of squib, let off by a slow-light and attached to its tail, as one by night. (Colonel Jackson.)

Sound. Whistling through the fingers can be heard at considerable distances; the accomplishment should be learnt. Cooing in the Australian fashion, or yodeling in that of the Swiss, are both of them heard a long way. The united *holloa* of many voices is heard much further than separate cries. The cracking of a whip has a very penetrating sound.

Smells. An abominable smell arrests the attention at night.

After graduating from Cambridge University, **Mansfield Parkyns** (British, 1823-94) departed on a journey to points east; after nine years' absence with no news of his whereabouts, he was presumed lost. Upon return to England he wrote a book of his adventures living among the peoples of Abyssinia, Nubia, Sennar, Kordofan, and Egypt. A contemporary biography of Parkyns is titled *The Gentleman Savage.*

☞ In short reconnoitering expeditions made by a small detachment from a party, the cattle or dogs are often wild and run home to their comrades on the first opportunity; in the event of not being able to watch them, owing to accident or other cause, advantage may be taken of their restlessness by tying a note to one of their necks, and letting them go and serve as postmen, or rather as carrier pigeons.

CACHES

BEST PLACE FOR A CACHE.

The best position to choose for a cache is in a sandy or gravelly soil, on account of its dryness and the facility of digging. Old burrows, or the gigantic but abandoned hills of white ants, may be thought of if the stores are enclosed in cases of painted tin; also clefts in rocks; some things can be conveniently buried under water. The place must be chosen under circumstances that admit of your effacing all signs of the ground having been disturbed.

A good plan is to set up your tent and to dig a deep hole in the floor, depositing what you have to bury wrapped in an oilcloth, in an earthen jar, or in a wooden vessel, according to what you are able to get. It must be secure against the attacks of the insects of the place; avoid the use of skins, for animals will smell and dig them out. Continue to inhabit the tent for at least a day, well stamping and smoothing down the soil at leisure. After this, change the position of the tent, shifting the tethering place or kraal of your cattle to where it stood. They will speedily efface any marks that may be left.

Newly disturbed ground sinks when wetted. If a cache be made in dry weather, and the ground be simply leveled over it, the first heavy rain will cause the earth to sink and will proclaim the hidden store to an observant eye. Soldiers, in sacking a town, find out hastily buried treasures by throwing a pailful of water over any suspected spot; if the ground sinks, it has surely been recently disturbed.

BEST PLACE FOR A CACHE.

DOUBLE CACHES.

SECRETING JEWELS.

☞ The natives in Ceylon, when they wish to make a depot of game, jerk it, put the dry meat into the hollow of a tree, fill up the reservoir with honey, and plaster it over with clay.

☞ Some dried plants of M. Bourgeau, the botanist attached to Captain Palliser's expedition to the Rocky Mountains, remained underground for ten months without injury.

☞ Travelers often make their fires over the holes where their stores are buried; but natives are so accustomed to suspect fireplaces that this plan does not prove to be safe.

☞ During summer travel, in countries pestered with gnats, a smoke fire for the horses (that is, a fire for keeping off flies) made near the place will attract the horses and cause them to trample all about. This is an excellent way of obliterating marks left about the cache.

Hiding small things. It is easy to make a small cache by bending down a young tree, tying your bundle to the top, and letting it spring up again. A spruce tree gives excellent shelter to anything placed in its branches.

Hiding large things. Large things, as a wagon or boat, must either be pushed into thick bushes or reeds and left to chance, or they may be buried in a sand drift or in a sandy deposit by a riverside. A small reedy island is a convenient place for such caches.

DOUBLE CACHES.

Some persons, when they know that their intentions are suspected, make two caches: the one with a few things buried in it and concealed with little care, the other containing those that are really valuable, and very artfully made. Thieves are sure to discover the first, and are likely enough to omit a further search.

To find your store again, you should have ascertained the distance and bearing, by compass, of the hole from some marked place—as a tree—about which you are sure not to be mistaken, or from the center of the place where your fire was made, which is a mark that years will not entirely efface. If there be anything in the ground itself to indicate the position of the hole, you have made a clumsy cache. It is not a bad plan, after the things are buried, and before the tent is removed, to scratch a furrow a couple of inches deep, and 3 or 4 feet long, and picking up any bits of stick, reeds, or straw that may be found at hand lying upon the ground, to place them end to end in it. These will be easy enough to find again by making a cross furrow, and when found will lead you straight above the depot. They would never excite suspicion, even if a native got hold of them, for they would appear to have been dropped or blown on the ground by chance, not seen, and trampled in.

SECRETING JEWELS.

Before going to a rich but imperfectly civilized country, travelers sometimes buy jewels and bury them in their flesh. They make a gash, put the jewels in, and allow the flesh to grow over them as it would over a bullet. The operation is more sure to succeed if the jewels are put into a silver tube with rounded ends, for silver does not irritate. If the jewels are buried without the tube, they must have no sharp edges. The best place for burying them is in the left arm at the spot chosen for vaccination. A traveler who was thus provided would always have a small capital to fall back upon, though robbed of everything he wore.

☞ Mr. Atkinson mentions an ingenious way by which the boundaries of valuable mining property are marked in the Ural, a modification of which might serve for indicating caches. A trench is dug and filled with charcoal beat small, and then covered over. The charcoal lasts forever, and cannot be tampered with without leaving an unmistakable mark.

☞ A chain of gold is sometimes carried by Arabs, who sew it in dirty leather under their belt. They cut off and sell a link at a time. (Burton.)

DRAWING LOTS.

PASSING THROUGH A HOSTILE
COUNTRY.

PROCEEDINGS IN CASE OF
DEATH.

KNOTS.

SEWING.

OTHER MATERIALS FOR
WRITING.

MAKESHIFT LIGHTING.

☞ Wherever you go, you
will find kindheartedness
amongst women. Mungo
Park ◈ is fond of recording
his experiences of this, but I
must add that he seems to
have been an especial favorite
with the sex. The gentler of
the two sexes is a "teterrima
causa belli."

MISCELLANY

DRAWING LOTS.

It is often necessary to distribute things by lot.
Do it by what children call "soldiering": one stands
with his back to the rest; another, pointing to the
portions in succession, calls out "Who is to have
this?" To which the first one replies by naming
somebody, who at once takes possession.

PASSING THROUGH A HOSTILE COUNTRY.

How to encamp. A small party has often occasion to try to steal through a belt of hostile country
without being observed. At such times, it is a rule
never to encamp until long after sundown, in order
that people on your track may be unable to pursue
it with ease. If you are pursuing a beaten path,
turn sharp out of it when you intend to encamp,
selecting a place for doing so where the ground is
too hard to show footprints; then travel away for
a quarter of an hour at least. Lastly, look out for a
hollow place in the midst of an open flat. Never allow hammering of any kind in your camp, nor loud
talking, but there is no danger in lighting a small fire
if reasonable precautions be taken, as a flame cannot
be seen far through bushes.

Keep a strict watch all night: the watchers should
be 100 yards out from camp, and should relieve one
another every two hours at least. Enough animals
for riding, one for each man, should always be tied
up in readiness for instant use.

When riding alone. A person who is riding a journey for his life, sleeps most safely with his horse's head tied short up to his wrist. The horse, if he hears anything, tosses his head and jerks the rider's arm. The horse is a careful animal, and there appears to be little danger of his treading on his sleeping master. The Indians of South America habitually adopt this plan when circumstances require extreme caution.

Head near the ground. When you think you hear anything astir, lie down and lay your ear on the ground. To see to the best advantage, take the same position; you thus bring low objects in bold relief against the sky. Besides this, in a wooded country, it is often easy to see far between the bare stems of the trees, while their spreading tops shut out all objects more than a few yards off. Thus a dog or other small animal usually sees a man's legs long before he sees his face.

Mungo Park (British, 1771-1806) is often described as "the distinguished but unfortunate Scottish traveler." Mungo was trained as a doctor and sailed to Sumatra as a ship's surgeon before turning to exploring. In 1795 he set out from Gambia on horseback, wearing a tall hat and carrying an umbrella, to follow the course of the Niger River. In an attack natives stole his umbrella, but Park hung onto his hat and kept the notes from his journey safe inside it, even during four months when he was held prisoner by Muslims. He returned to England and became an instant celebrity upon publication of his *Travels in the Interior Districts of Africa.* Park led a full-scale expedition back to the Niger and the near-mythical city of Timbuktu in 1805, and of the forty Europeans who took part in the ill-fated trip, none survived it. After traveling nearly 1,000 miles on the river, Park drowned in an attack on the Bussa Rapids.

PROCEEDINGS IN CASE OF DEATH.

If a man of the party dies, write down a detailed account of the matter and have it attested by the others, especially if accident be the cause of his death. If a man be lost, before you turn away and abandon him to his fate, call the party formally together and ask them if they are satisfied that you have done all that was possible to save him, and record their answers.

After death, it is well to follow the custom at sea—i.e., to sell by auction all the dead man's effects among his comrades, deducting the money they fetch from the pay of the buyers, to be handed over to his relatives on the return of the expedition. The things will probably be sold at a much higher price than they would elsewhere fetch, and the carriage of useless lumber is saved. Any trinkets he may have had should of course be sealed up and put aside, and not included in the sale: they should be collected in presence of the whole party, a list made of them, and the articles at once packed up.

In committing the body to the earth, choose a well-marked situation, dig a deep grave, bush it with thorns, and weight it well over with heavy stones, as a defense against animals of prey.

KNOTS.

The three elementary knots which every one should know are here represented—viz., the timber hitch, the bowline, and the clove hitch.

Timber hitch. The virtues of the timber hitch *(fig. 1)* are that, so long as the strain upon it is kept up, it will hold fast; when the strain is taken off, it can

Any trinkets he may have had should of course be sealed up and put aside

Fig. 1

be cast loose immediately. A timber hitch had better have the loose end twisted more than once if the rope be stiff.

Bowline. The bowline *(fig. 2)* makes a knot difficult to undo; with it the ends of two strings are tied together, or a loop made at the end of a single piece of string as in the drawing. For slip nooses, use the bowline to make the draw-loop. When tying a bowline or any other knot for temporary purposes, insert a stick into the knot before pulling tight. The stick will enable you, at will, to untie the knot—to break its back, as the sailors say—with little difficulty. A bowline is firmer if doubled; that is, if the free end of the cord be made to wrap round a second time.

Fig.2

Clove hitch. The clove hitch *(fig. 3)* binds with excessive force, and by it and it alone can a weight be hung to a perfectly smooth pole, as to a tent-pole. A kind of double clove hitch is generally used, but the simple one suffices and is more easily recollected. A double clove hitch is firmer than a single one; that is, the rope should make two turns, instead of one turn, round the pole beneath the lowest end of the cord in the figure.

Fig. 3

SEWING.

The enthusiastic traveler should be thoroughly grounded by a tailor in the rudiments of sewing and the most useful stitches. They are as follows: to make a knot at the end of the thread; to run; to stitch; to "sew"; to fell, or otherwise to make a double seam; to herring-bone (essential for flannels); to hem; to sew over; to bind; to sew on a button; to make a button hole; to darn; and to fine-draw. He should also practice taking patterns of some articles of clothing in paper, cutting them out in common materials and putting them together. He should take a lesson or two from a saddler, and several, when on board ship, from a sailmaker.

OTHER MATERIALS FOR WRITING.

Quills and other pens. Any feather that is large enough can be at once made into a good writing quill. It has only to be dipped in hot sand, which causes the membrane inside the quill to shrivel up and the outside membrane to split and peel off; a few instants are sufficient to do this. The proper temperature of the sand is about 340°. The operation may be repeated two or three times. Reeds are in universal use throughout the East for writing with ink. Flat fish bones make decent pens.

Ink. Excellent writing ink may be made in the bush. The readiest way of making it is to blacken sticks in the fire and to rub them well in a spoonful of milk till the milk becomes quite black. Gunpowder or lamp soot will do as well as the burnt stick, and water with the addition of a very little gum, glue, or fish glue is better than the milk, as it will not so soon turn sour. Indian ink is simply lamp soot and some kind of glue; it is one of the best of inks. If pure water be used, the writing will rub out very easily when dry, the use of the milk, gum, or glue being to fix it; anything else that is glutinous will serve as well as these. Strong coffee and many other vegetable products, such as the bark of trees boiled in water, make a mark which is very legible and will not rub. Blood is a poor substitute for ink.

☞ Sympathetic ink: nothing is better or handier than milk. The writing is invisible until the paper is almost toasted in the fire, when it turns a rich brown. The juice of lemons and many other fruits may also be used.

Substitutes for paper are chips of wood, inner bark of trees, calico and other tissues, lead plates, and slatey stone. I knew an eminent engineer who habitually jotted his pencil memoranda on the well-starched wristband of his left shirtsleeve, pushing back the cuff of his coat in order to expose it. The natives in some parts of Bengal, when in the jungle, write on any large smooth leaf with the broken-off moist end of a leafstalk or twig of any milky sap-producing tree. They then throw dust upon it, which makes the writing legible. If the leaf be so written upon, the writing is imperceptible until the dust is sprinkled. This plan might, therefore, be of use for concealed writing. A person could write on the leaf without detaching it from the tree.

MAKESHIFT LIGHTING.

Substitute for candles. A strip of cotton, 1½ foot long, drenched in grease and wound spirally round a wand, will burn for half an hour. A lump of beeswax, with a tatter of an old handkerchief run through it, makes a candle on an emergency.

Candlestick. A hole cut with the knife in a sod of turf or a potato; three, four, or five nails hammered in a circle into a piece of wood, to act as a socket; a hollow bone; an empty bottle; a strap with the end passed the wrong way through the buckle and coiled inside; and a bayonet stuck in the ground, are all used as makeshift candlesticks.

In bygone days the broad feet, or rather legs, of the swan, after being stretched and dried, were converted into candlesticks. (Lloyd. ◈)

Llewellyn Lloyd (British) was the father of Charles Andersson, second-in-command on Galton's expedition in southwest Africa. Lloyd was the author of numerous books on hunting and wildlife. In his autobiography, Galton writes, "I made Mr. Lloyd's acquaintance some years later, when his face had been frightfully scarred with wounds made by a bear. He told me that an old wounded she-bear had turned upon him, and actually got his head between her jaws to crack it, but her rounded teeth failed to find at once a sufficiently sharp hold and only tore the flesh. His companion shot the animal in time."

Lantern. A wooden box, a native bucket, or a calabash will make the frame, and a piece of greased calico stretched across a hole in its side will take the place of glass. A small tin, such as a preserved-meat case, makes a good lantern if a hole is broken into the bottom and an opening in the side or front. Horn is easily to be worked by a traveler into any required shape. A good and often a ready makeshift for a lantern is a bottle with its end cracked off. This is best effected by putting water into the bottle to the depth of an inch and then setting it upon hot embers. The bottle will crack all round at the level of the top of the water. It takes a strong wind to blow out a candle stuck into the neck inside the broken bottle. Alpine tourists often employ this contrivance when they start from their bivouac in the dark morning.

ON CONCLUDING THE JOURNEY

COMPLETE YOUR COLLECTIONS.

When your journey draws near its close, resist restless feelings; make every effort before it is too late to supplement deficiencies in your various collection; take stock of what you have gathered together, and think how the things will serve in England to illustrate your journey or your book. Keep whatever is pretty in itself, or is illustrative of your everyday life, or that of the savages, in the way of arms, utensils, and dresses. Make careful drawings of your encampment, your retinue, and whatever else you may in indolence have omitted to sketch, that will possess an after-interest. Look over your vocabularies for the last time, and complete them as far as possible. Make presents of all your traveling gear and old guns to your native attendants, for they will be mere litter in England, costly to house and attractive to moth and rust; while in the country where you have been traveling they are of acknowledged value and would be additionally acceptable as keepsakes.

MEMORANDA, TO ARRANGE.

Paste all loose slips of MSS. into the pages of a blank book and stitch your memoranda books where they are torn; give them to a bookbinder, at the first opportunity, to re-bind and page them, adding an abundance of blank leaves. Write an index to the whole of your MSS.; put plenty of cross references, insert necessary explanations, and

COMPLETE YOUR COLLECTIONS.

MEMORANDA, TO ARRANGE.

ALPHABETICAL LISTS.

VERIFICATION OF INSTRUMENTS.

OBSERVATIONS, TO RECALCULATE.

LITHOGRAPH MAPS.

Make presents of all your traveling gear and old guns to your native attendants, for they will be mere litter in England

Crowds of new impressions, during a few months or years of civilized life, will efface the sharpness of the old ones

supplement imperfect descriptions, while your memory of the events remains fresh. It appears impossible to a traveler, at the close of his journey, to believe he will ever forget its events, however trivial, for after long brooding on few facts, they will seem to be fairly branded into his memory. But this is not the case, for the crowds of new impressions, during a few months or years of civilized life, will efface the sharpness of the old ones. I have conversed with men of low mental power, servants and others, the greater part of whose experiences in savagedom had passed out of their memories like the events of a dream.

ALPHABETICAL LISTS.

Every explorer has frequent occasion to draw up long catalogues in alphabetical order, whether of words for vocabularies, or of things that he has in store; now, there is a right and a wrong way of setting to work to make them. The wrong way is to divide the paper into equal parts and to assign one of them to each letter in order. The right way is to divide the paper into parts of a size proportionate to the number of words in the English language which begin with each particular letter. In the first case the paper will be overcrowded in some parts and utterly blank in others, in the second it will be equally overspread with writing; and an ordinary-sized sheet of paper, if closely and clearly written, will be sufficient for the drawing up of a very extended catalogue.

A convenient way of carrying out the principle I have indicated is to take an English dictionary, and after having divided the paper into as many equal parts as there are leaves in the dictionary, to adopt the first word of each leaf as headings to them. It may save trouble to my reader if I give a list of headings appropriate to a small catalogue. We will suppose the paper to be divided into fifty-two spaces—that is to say, into four columns and thirteen spaces in each column—and the headings of these spaces, in order, will be as follows:

A	dul	pal	son
adv	eve	per	sta
app	fin	ple	sir
bal	gin	pre	sur
bil	hee	pro	tem
bre	imp	que	tos
cap	int	rec	tur
chi	k	reg	umb
col	lan	ris	une
com	mac	sab	ven
cra	mil	sca	wea
dec	nap	sha	wor
dis	off	siz	x y z

VERIFICATION OF INSTRUMENTS.

On arriving at the sea level, make daily observations with your boiling-point thermometer, barometer, and aneroid, as they are all subject to changes in their index errors. As soon as you have an opportunity, compare them with a standard barometer, compare also your ordinary thermometer and azimuth compass with standard instruments, and finally, have them carefully re-verified at the Kew observatory on your return to England. A vast deal of labor has been wholly thrown away by travelers owing to their neglecting to ascertain the index errors of these instruments at the close of their journey.

OBSERVATIONS, TO RECALCULATE.

Send by post to England a complete copy (always preserve the originals) of all your astronomical observations, that they may be carefully recalculated before your return; otherwise a long period may elapse before the longitudes are finally settled, and your book may be delayed through the consequent impossibility of preparing a correct map. The Royal Geographical Society has frequently procured the re-calculation of observations made on important journeys, at the Royal Greenwich Observatory and elsewhere. I presume that a well-known traveler would never find a difficulty in obtaining the calculations he might desire through the medium of that Society, if it was distinctly understood that they were to be made at his own cost.

LITHOGRAPH MAPS.

It may add greatly to the interest which a traveler will take in drawing up a large and graphic route-map of his journey, if he knows the extreme ease and cheapness with which copies of such a map may be multiplied to any extent by lithography: for these being distributed among persons interested in the country where he has traveled will prevent his painstaking from being lost to the world. Sketches and bird's-eye views may be multiplied in the same manner. A map drawn on a large scale, though without any pretension to artistic skill, with abundance of profile views of prominent landmarks, and copious information upon the routes that were explored written along their sides, would be of the utmost value to future travelers and to geographers at home.

INDEX

PERSONAGES.

[Bold-face page numbers indicate a thumbnail biography inserted by the editor]

Alexander the Great, 54
Amundsen, Roald, 27
Andersson, Charles John, **53**, 75
Atkinson, Thomas Witlam, **88**, 163
Baker, Samuel, 20, 76, 84, **87**
Ballantyne, Robert Michael, **79**
Barclay-Allardice, Robert, **136**
Barth, Heinrich, **18**, 59
Beke, Charles Tilstone, 84, **85**
Blakiston, Thomas Wright, 38
Bligh, William, **26**, 83
Borrow, George Henry, **150**
Bourgeau, M., 161
Bruce, James, **84**, 85
Burke, Robert O'Hara, **78**
Burton, Richard Francis, 18, **29**, 112, 163
Caesar, Julius, 133
Campbell, Mr., 104
Catlin, George, 81
Cheadle, Walter, 152
Cooper, W.M., 133
Crawfurd, Mr., 89
Crusoe, Robinson, **55**
Cumming, R. Gordon, 98, **100**
Dalyell, R., 65
Darwin, Charles, 31, 58, 107
Defoe, Daniel, 55
Douglas, Howard, **66**
Euler, Leonhard, 29
Everest, George, **143**
Eyre, Edward John, 74, **102**
Falconer, Thomas, **118**
FitzRoy, Robert, 57, **58**
Fitzwilliam, William Wentworth *(see Milton)*
Fremont, John Charles, **56**, 57

Gabet, Joseph, 32
Galton, Francis, 21, 53, 121
Gardiner, Allen, **78**
Garibaldi, Giuseppe, 19
Glaisher, James, **121**
Gilby, Mr., 61, 97
Hawker, Peter, 94
Hearne, Samuel, **15**
Hooker, Joseph Dalton, **125**, 150
Huber, Pierre, 146, **147**
Hue, Evariste, **32**
Jackson, Julian, **39**, 160
Kane, Elisha Kent, 94, 126, 137, 151, **154**
Laird, MacGregor, **60**
Lefroy, John Henry, **54**, 59
Leichhardt, Friedrich Wilhelm Ludwig, **68**, 85
Livingstone, David, 21, **57**, 125
Lloyd, Llewellyn, 93, **169**
Matonabbee, 15
Milton, Viscount, **152**
Moffat, Robert, **125**
Murray, Charles Augustus, **109**
Murray III, John, **137**
Napoleon Bonaparte, 120, 126, 127, 153
Owen, Prof., 93
Oswell, William Cotton, **21**
Palliser, 25, 59, **95**, 161
Park, Mungo, 31, 164, **165**
Parkyns, Mansfield, 25, 137, **160**
Pereira, Mr., 81
Rae, John, 26, **27**, 75
Rarey, John Solomon, **30**
Richardson, James, **59**
Rumford, Count, **20**, 21
St. John, Mr., 99, 126
Schlagintweit, Adolf, Eduard, Emil, Hermann, and Robert, 34, **35**, 136
Shaw, Mr., 121, 122
Speke, John Hanning, 29
Spottiswoode, William, **150**
Stanley, Henry, 57

Sullivan, Mr., 158
Thompson, Benjamin *(see Rumford)*
Tyndall, Prof., 21
Von Tschudi, Johann Jakob, **102**, 136
Von Wrangel, Ferdinand, **34**
Wills, William John, **78**
Woolley, Mr., 40

PLACES AND PEOPLES.

Abyssinia (Ethiopia), 84, 99, 160
Adrianople, p. 107
Africa, 11, 29, 75, 87, 92, 100, 105, 107, 137, 160
Alaska, 34
Aliab (Sudan), 83
Alps, 136, 146
Amalfi, 24
Andorre (France), 117
Angra Pequena (Namibia), 74
Antarctica, 125
Arabia, 29, 76, 163
Arctic regions, 27, 34, 57, 72, 75, 79, 121
Armenia, 107
Asia, 29
Assam (India), 71
Australia, 11, 16, 68, 75, 78, 93, 101, 125, 137, 160
Barren Grounds (Canada), 15
Bedouin, 89
Bengal (Bangladesh and India), 71, 169
Bermuda, 54
Bornu (Nigeria), 54, 130
Brazil, 60, 102
Bushmen (S. Africa), 77
California, 56
Canada, 15, 36, 54, 79, 95, 107, 152
Caribbean, 26
Ceylon (Sri Lanka), 87, 129, 161
Chamonix (France), 24
Chagre, 25
Channel Islands, 107

China, 33, 85, 88, 105
Chippewa, 15
Central Africa, 18, 87
Congo River, 57
Cree,
East Africa, 29
Egypt, 61, 97, 109, 160
England, 30, 129
Erzurum (Turkey), 65
Eskimo, 89, 94, 137
Ethiopia, 85
Europe, 27
Falkland Islands, 107
Faroe Islands (Denmark), 40
Flamborough Head
    (England), 40
Foula Island (Shetland), 40
France, 77, 117
Gambia, 165
Germany, 23, 118
Great Salt Lake, 57
Gypsies (Romany), 129
Himalaya, 71, 136, 143
Hindu, 101
Hudson Bay, 15
India, 29, 108, 125, 133, 142,
    143
Inuit,
Italy, 61
Jamaica, 102
Komadugu River (Nigeria),
    54
Krumen (Liberia), 63
Kuruman (S. Africa), 125
Lake Ngami, 53
Lake Chad, 60
Lake Tanganyika, 57
Lake Titicaca, 57
Libya, 18
Mackenzie River, 15, 59
Mandan (N. American tribe),
    81
Maori (New Zealand), 132
Mediterranean Sea, 60
Mexico, 118
Mount Idinen, 18
Mohammedan (Muslim),
    27, 67

Mongolia, 88
Morocco, 125
Muslims, 165
Namaqua Land, 35
Namibia, 53
New Holland (Australia), 26
New Mexico, 118
New Zealand, 39, 102, 132
Niger River, 60, 80, 165
Nile River, 29, 57, 84, 85
North Africa, 16, 18, 32, 81
North America, 16, 38, 75, 80,
    109, 139, 152, 158
Norway, 56, 61
Oregon Territory, 56
Orinoco River (Columbia,
    Venezuela), 55
Otago (New Zealand), 132
Ovampo (Namibia), 111
Palestine, 125
Paraguay, 87
Paris, 83
Patagonia, 78, 105
Pawnee, 109
Persia (Iran), 133
Peru, 102
Pyrenees, 24, 117
Rocky Mountains, 161
Russia, 81, 88, 149, 150, 163
Sahara Desert, 59, 60, 130
St. Kilda (Hebrides), 40
Sancerre (France), 83
Scotland, 100, 116, 136
Sebastapol (Ukraine), 129
Shire River (Malawi,
    Mozambique), 85
Siberia, 16, 34, 88, 146

Sikkim (India), 71
Snake River, 77
South Africa, 16, 21, 81, 98,
    125
Southern Africa, 53, 84
South America, 16, 58, 102,
    105, 136, 165
Spain, 95
Spitsbergen (Norway, Russia),
    81
Sulu (Philippines), 61
Sumatra, 165
Sweden, 62, 93, 101, 124
Switzerland, 102, 146, 148,
    160
Tahiti, 26
Tambov (Russia), 149
Tasmania, 54
Texas, 118
Tibet, 32, 107, 121, 122, 125
Tierra del Fuego, 78
Timbuktu,
Tigris River, 54
Timor, 26
Tioughe River (S. Africa), 53
Tripoli, 59
United States, 36, 56, 92,
    118, 125
Unyoro (Central Africa), 20,
    76, 87
Ural (Russia), 163
Victoria Falls, 57
Vidin (Bulgaria), 87
Westmaroer Islands (Iceland),
    40
Yoruba (West Africa), 48
Zambezi River (southern
    Africa), 57

LETTER BURIED
50 yards N.N.E.

1 Under- stood.	2 Not understood.	A 5	3 Numeral.	4 Wait.
B 6	C 7	D 8	E 9	F 10
G 11	H 12	I 13	J 14	K 15
L 16	M 17	N 18	O 19	P 20
Q 21	R 22	S 23	T 24	U 25
V 26	W 27	X 28	Y 29	Z 30

Fig. 3.